TRUTH
FOR
ALL
TIME

Great Gospel
Words

Colin N Peckham

Day One

© Day One Publications 2008
First printed 2008

ISBN 978–1–84625–138–2

British Library Cataloguing in Publication Data available

Published by Day One Publications
Ryelands Road, Leominster, HR6 8NZ
☎ 01568 613 740 FAX 01568 611 473
email—sales@dayone.co.uk
web site—www.dayone.co.uk
North American—e-mail—sales@dayonebookstore.com
North American—web site—www.dayonebookstore.com

Cover design by Wayne McMaster
Printed by Gutenberg Press, Malta

This further work from the pen of Dr Colin Peckham on 'great gospel words' is most welcome, especially at a time when the average church member has no real understanding of the essential elements of the gospel.

Today, when few Christians would take the time to read a volume of systematic theology, perhaps this will be the ideal medium to help them to reach a clearer view of what they believe and profess in terms of the gospel. It is excellent material in a concise and readable form and I trust it will have a wide readership.

Revd Tom Shaw BA. MTh
Congregational minister, Northern Ireland,
and former President of the Faith Mission

In an age of increasing biblical illiteracy, here is a book which unpacks and explains the key words and themes which underpin the gospel. Written by an experienced pastor and theologian, Dr Colin Peckham, it will be a valuable resource for those just discovering the riches that are in Christ, as well as a fresh encouragement to those who have mined them for many years. And it is so easy to read!

Revd Peter J. Grainger
Senior Pastor, Charlotte Baptist Chapel, Edinburgh

Contents

Dedication

I dedicate this book to the students whom I taught in the past and to those

who study at present at the two Bible colleges where I was privileged to be

Principal, and to lovers of God's Word everywhere.

Introduction

Many people in our churches today do not understand the basic doctrines of salvation and cannot easily distinguish between the different aspects of God's plan of deliverance and salvation. These studies are designed to help us all to understand the different features and parts of the whole.

'Salvation' is a broad word that incorporates all the aspects of salvation, while 'repentance', 'justification', 'regeneration' and 'assurance' are parts of the whole message. Without repentance, there will be no justification, that aspect that takes place when the Lord speaks me free as I stand condemned before the bar of God. Regeneration occurs when God's Spirit enters my being and makes me his child. The whole experience of salvation brings great assurance to the trusting soul. In this book, the salvation event is dealt with in its separate aspects.

These studies are not merely academic; they also bring the challenge of an encounter with the God who made this salvation possible. The book is designed to instruct and educate, guide and enlighten, confront and persuade, as well as to stimulate appreciation, inspiration and wonder at God's great salvation. For those who preach and teach, this book contains valuable source material. For those who have a limited understanding of the subject of salvation, this book should bring light and clarity of thought. For those who have not yet experienced God's salvation, this book can open their minds and draw them to the One who gives eternal life in Christ Jesus.

May God use it to his glory.

Dr Colin N. Peckham LTh(Hons), BA(Theol), BTh(Hons), MTh, DTh
Edinburgh, 2008

Salvation: deliverance from sin

Definitions of salvation

- 'Salvation is the most widely used term in Christian theology to express the provision of God for our human plight. It is used in a very broad sense of the sum total of the effects of God's goodness on his people' (*New Dictionary of Theology*).[1]
- 'Salvation is the comprehensive term to describe the complete deliverance that God, through the person and work of Christ, and by the operation of the Holy Spirit, gives to his people. It includes all the other soteriological terms' (*Dictionary of Theological Terms*).[2]
- 'The root idea of salvation is deliverance from danger or evil. Salvation is represented primarily in the NT as deliverance from sin. It is both present and eschatological. It is not only deliverance from future punishment, but also from sin as a present power. It includes all the redemption blessings we have in Christ' (*Zondervan's Pictorial Bible Dictionary*).[3]
- 'Salvation always signifies deliverance from enemies or from dangers. In the New Testament it takes on a profounder meaning—deliverance from the thraldom of sin' (*G. Henderson*).[4]
- 'God's offer of salvation includes more than the acceptance of the words and the ethically impeccable life of his Son; it demands submission to Christ's cross. The salvation which God offers mankind is realizable only through the cross of Christ' (*God, Man and Salvation*).[5]
- 'Salvation denotes simply "deliverance" in almost any sense the latter word can have. In systematic theology, however, "salvation" denotes the whole process by which man is delivered from all that would prevent his attaining to the highest good that God has prepared for him. Or, by a transferred sense, "salvation" denotes the actual

enjoyment of that good' (*International Standard Bible Encyclopedia*).[6]

- 'The New Testament indicates clearly man's thraldom to sin ... and the deliverance from it to be found exclusively in Christ ... God provides the basis for salvation, presents it, and is himself man's salvation' (*The New Bible Dictionary*).[7]

The need for salvation

The subject of salvation demands careful study and clear understanding, for it is the central theme of the Scriptures. 'Christ Jesus came into the world to save sinners' (1 Tim. 1:15); 'the Son of Man has come to seek and to save that which was lost' (Luke 19:10); Joseph was told to call Mary's son 'JESUS, for He will save His people from their sins' (Matt. 1:21).

If the mission of Christ provides the only way to God, and if God's judgements fall on all who do not accept this salvation, is it not imperative to know what the Bible teaches about this all-important subject? Does the Bible not warn us that we shall not escape if we neglect this salvation (Heb. 2:3)?

Before we look at the wonderfully enriching elements of this salvation, we need to consider the condition of the heart of man which makes God's salvation necessary.

Sin has entered the human race as a vile intruder (Rom. 5:12). It originated with the devil, who deceived man into deliberately disobeying God. It is an inward corruption which shows itself in wicked thoughts, words and actions (Rom. 3:10–18). It is a loathsome quality, dominating man like a tyrant and holding man in its wearisome bondage (Rom. 7:14–20). Its evil has spread through man's nature, leaving no part untouched, and it mercilessly drags him downwards (Eph. 2:2–3). Its repulsive carnal mind schemes enmity against God (Rom. 8:5–8). To the natural man, sin's carnality is ungovernable; its rebellion is perennial; its lawlessness is unconquerable. Man's understanding is darkness and his imagination is depraved. Sin's wickedness has ruined his life and distorted his nature. His heart is deceitful and desperately wicked (Jer. 17:9). The mind and conscience are defiled. The will is enfeebled and enslaved. The entire nature of man—mentally, spiritually and physically—has been affected by sin. Man is perverted and totally depraved. His sin has separated him from God (Isa. 59:2). He has missed his true aim in life. The tragedy is that the whole human race is affected. All are poisoned and polluted; all are in this dreadful predicament: 'all have sinned and fall short of the glory of God' (Rom. 3:23). All are guilty and therefore destined for punishment, for God has said, 'The soul who sins shall die' (Ezek. 18:4).

Man is guilt-laden and totally unfit for heaven. He is under the awful wrath of a holy God (John 3:36). There is no escape but only the certain prospect of damnation and death (Rom. 1:18). The judgement of God will certainly fall on those who do not know him (2 Thes. 1:7–9).

Because man's moral integrity has been forfeited, right action is impossible and he is utterly unable to save himself. He is blind and cannot find his way back to God; he is without strength and cannot work his way back to God; his will is perverted and he cannot will his way back to God; he is spiritually dead and he cannot generate life in order to find God (Eph. 4:18; Rom. 5:6). He is bound by Satan, 'having been taken captive by him to do his will' (2 Tim. 2:26), and he cannot free himself from bondage; he is defiled and cannot cleanse himself from sin. He is without hope apart from a saving act of divine grace (Eph. 2:12). Man needs salvation.

The source of salvation

The Bible leaves us in no doubt as to the source of man's salvation. It is God who conceived it in the dateless past and in his eternal purposes. Salvation was no afterthought: man's sin did not take God by surprise and force him hastily to create an emergency escape route for the sinner. God planned this salvation before man was created, so that when man fell, as God knew he would, the plan of salvation was already there for his eternal benefit (Rev. 13:8). God tells us that he 'saved us ... according to His own purpose and grace which was given to us in Christ Jesus before time began' (2 Tim. 1:9).

God is spoken of as a Saviour who saves with 'everlasting salvation' (Isa. 45:15,17). He invites men to 'Look to Me, and be saved, all you ends of the earth! For I am God, and there is no other' (Isa. 45:22). Jehovah is presented as Saviour throughout the Old Testament. In the New Testament, the Son executes the saving plan of which the Father is the architect. Christ is the 'author' and 'source' of our salvation (NIV: Heb. 2:10; Heb. 5:9). In fact, he *is* our salvation, and has been raised for our salvation in the house of David (Isa. 49:6; Luke 1:69). He has it, and he brings it with him (Zech. 9:9; Isa. 62:11; Luke 19:9). He came to effect salvation (Matt. 18:11). He died for that purpose and is now mighty to execute, and exalted to give, God's great salvation (John 3:14–15; Isa. 63:1; Heb. 7:25; Acts 5:31). He came into the world to seek and to save sinners (Luke 19:10; 1 Tim. 1:15). He was called 'Jesus' because of his mission to save (Matt. 1:21). In fact, there is no other name by which salvation may be procured (Acts 4:12).

Man has sinned, and Christ's death, as an act of atonement for sin, is necessary to restore the broken relationship between a holy God and sinful man. God's righteousness demands punishment but his love provides the substitute. Christ took our sins and bore our punishment when he offered the sacrifice of infinite and eternal value at Calvary and there paid the penalty for sin (Isa. 53:4–6,10,12). Christ takes the sin away from the transgressor, who is then considered justified from all unrighteousness and cleansed from all defilement. God's righteous character has been maintained in that he has punished the One who has identified himself with the sin. Because of that punishment, man is offered salvation and fellowship with God. God can be gracious without being unjust in welcoming sinful man. Salvation for man is accomplished.

The scope of salvation

'Salvation' is an inclusive word, gathering together all the redemptive acts and processes such as grace, justification, sanctification and glorification. Being saved from sin and from the wrath of God is necessary and basic, but it is only the initial feature of salvation (Rom. 5:9).

Salvation includes the aspect of redemption, where the thought is of buying people back from the bondage of sin. The word 'redemption' comes from the slave market, where the slave's release was secured by paying the ransom price. Peter tells us, however, that we 'were not redeemed with corruptible things, like silver or gold' (1 Peter 1:18). No earthly means could secure our freedom; only the precious blood of Christ was sufficient to release us from sin's degrading bondage (Heb. 9:12; Titus

2:14). We were all slaves of Satan, sold under sin, but Christ became our ransom and set us free (Matt. 20:28; 1 Tim. 2:6; 1 Cor. 6:19–20).

Man revolted against God and has become his enemy, yet it is God, the offended party, who takes the initiative in providing the atonement for man's reconciliation. He ordains the atoning sacrifice and gives his Son as an offering for mankind (Rom. 5:10; Col. 1:21). In fact, 'God was in Christ, reconciling the world to Himself' (2 Cor. 5:19; see also v.18). Though his majesty is offended by man's sin, and his holiness has to react against it, God is not willing that the sinner should perish, so he did something to reconcile man to himself. The act of reconciliation is a completed work (Heb. 10:10).

Christ's death has made the reconciliation of sinners possible and each individual, by receiving that death, makes it actual.

A beautiful aspect of salvation is that of the sovereign God forgiving the rebel—the aspect of remission. The blood of Christ was poured out 'for the remission of sins' (Matt. 26:28). The Old Testament offering secured forgiveness for the worshipper (Heb. 9:22); how much more the offering of Christ (Heb. 9:28)! There is 'redemption through His blood, the forgiveness of sins' (Eph. 1:7); 'through this Man [Jesus] is preached to you the forgiveness of sins' (Acts 13:38).

In wonder lost, with trembling joy,
We take the pardon from our God:
Pardon for sins of deepest dye,
A pardon sealed with Jesus' blood.
Who is a pardoning God like thee?
Or who has grace so rich and free?
(Samuel Davies, 1723–1761).

No longer do our consciences accuse us; no longer do our sinful pasts hang like dead weights upon us, for our sins are blotted out, taken away, forgotten. We are free!

The aspect of salvation which has to do with the legal relationships is that of justification. Sinners are summoned before the court of divine justice and, amazingly, they are honourably discharged, although proven guilty of all the charges laid against them. Condemnation is changed to justification because another Person has taken the punishment for the crimes committed. The sinners are allowed to go free just as if they had never sinned. Christ has done what was totally unmerited, unprompted and unsought: he accepted the Judge's verdict and died as our substitute. The grounds of our justification lie in his blood, and the principle of our justification is faith (Rom. 5:9,1). Justification is that judicial act whereby God, on account of a new faith relationship with Jesus Christ, declares sinners to be no longer exposed to the penalty of a broken law, but restored to divine favour. Sinners are acquitted and declared righteous. Our justification depends wholly on God and not on anything in ourselves.

At Calvary we see what Christ has done for us. The consequences of Calvary are known as we experience what he does in us. Not only does he forgive our sins, but he also possesses our lives by the Holy Spirit. Justification gives us a cleansed record; regeneration gives us a new nature: we become 'partakers of the divine nature', thus being made entirely new (2 Peter 1:4; 2 Cor. 5:7). This is not merely an improvement of the old nature, a mere reformation; rather it is the possessing of a new life that we could never develop in ourselves. The life of God is imparted and we are born of God. This new life brings with it a new nature with new aspirations, longings, hopes and plans. There is a new standing and a new destiny, for we are now children of the living God.

The three stages of salvation: past, present and future

Not only is it true to say 'I have been saved', but we must also realize that we are *being* saved and will *finally be* saved. God's perfect salvation covers the past, includes the present and embraces the future. The moment we accept Christ as Saviour, we receive the gift of God's salvation. We are then saved from the penalty of our sins, and in this sense we can say that we *have been* saved.

Yet salvation is that in which we presently rejoice. We are 'clothed' with and satisfied by our salvation (Isa. 61:10; Luke 2:30). We 'rejoice' in it (Ps. 9:14); we 'glory' in it (1 Cor. 1:30–31); and we 'tell' of this salvation which we have through grace and which beautifies our lives (Ps. 71:15; Gal. 6:14;

Ps. 40:10; Acts 15:11; Ps. 149:4). We are assured that 'now is the day of salvation' (2 Cor. 6:2). The question is whether or not we are experiencing present salvation. Are we trusting God constantly to keep us clean and to be giving us victory in our daily lives? Is ours the overcoming life? Are we not called to a holy life (2 Tim. 1:9)? And are we not chosen 'for salvation through sanctification by the Spirit' (2 Thes. 2:13)?

There is, however, a yet more wonderful aspect of salvation to consider, for not only is salvation past and present, it is also future. We look forward to the further communication of it all when we will be saved, not only from the penalty and power of sin, but also, when Jesus returns, at last from its very presence.

At the moment we are heirs of this final salvation (Heb. 1:14). We are saved by 'hope' as we 'wait' and long for its revelation (Rom. 8:24; Lam. 3:26). We earnestly look for it, and daily approach nearer to it (Ps. 119:123; Rom. 13:11). Peter says that the 'end of your faith' is 'the salvation of your souls' (1 Peter 1:9) and that we are 'kept by the power of God through faith for salvation ready to be revealed in the last time' (1 Peter 1:5). One day, we, together with many others, will hear a loud voice in heaven saying, 'Now salvation, and strength, and the kingdom of our God ... have come' (Rev. 12:10). Then salvation will be experienced in its final form 'with eternal glory' and we will be with our Saviour for ever (2 Tim. 2:10).

The communication of salvation

The gospel message of saving grace which sets people free from sin is found in the Bible, but it is only effective in those who receive that message by faith.

Paul assures Timothy that the 'Holy Scriptures' are able to make him 'wise for salvation through faith', and James urges his readers to 'receive with meekness the implanted word, which is able to save your souls' (2 Tim. 3:15; James 1:21). Paul states that it is by the gospel that 'you are saved' (1 Cor. 15:1–2). In fact, the gospel is 'the power of God to salvation for everyone who believes' (Rom. 1:16); 'it pleased God through the foolishness of the message preached to save those who believe' (1 Cor. 1:21).

Preaching is a manifestation of the incarnate Word, from the written word by the spoken word. It is truth expressed through personality, and this truth speaks to the whole person. It touches every aspect of what a person knows, feels and does: the mind, emotions and will. The message is from God, but it must be moulded into shape by the preacher and presented in such a way that it will reach the minds and hearts of the hearers and achieve the purpose for which it was intended.

The appeal of the gospel message enlightens the intellect with clear statements, logical arguments and well-applied conclusions. The emotions are stirred by the biblical revelation of the awfulness of sin and the wonderful story of a dying Saviour's love. The will is the last aspect to yield, but the bold, faithful and authoritative proclamation of the gospel captures the will and results in its full consent. There is an unconditional surrender. The hearer is intellectually convinced, morally convicted and spiritually converted. The word of the gospel has been the means of salvation.

This is clear in Paul's letter to the Ephesians: 'In Him you also trusted, after you heard the word of truth, the gospel of your salvation' (Eph. 1:13). The 'word of truth' which they heard from the lips of the apostle was the gospel of their salvation. The communication of the gospel, the proclamation of the 'word of truth', is very closely linked to the truth itself; indeed, as that truth is proclaimed, it has saving power. Preaching is a demonstration of Christ's presence and man's salvation. It is the radiation, application and extension of Christ's great work of salvation, the means by which this salvation is brought to the hearts of those who savingly believe, transforming them for ever.

Some, however, do not believe and, even though they have heard, are not saved; the message they heard was of no value to them because it was not 'mixed with faith' (Heb. 4:2). 'How then shall they call on Him in whom they have not believed? And how shall they believe in Him of whom they have not heard? And how shall they hear without a preacher? ... So then faith comes by hearing, and hearing by the word of God' (Rom. 10:14,17).

The eternal word of God must be preached by redeemed man so that others may hear, trust and experience God's great salvation.

The characteristics of salvation

There are many different characteristics of salvation, some of which are as follows:

SALVATION IS SHARED

Salvation is called our 'common salvation' (Jude 3). It is a salvation we share together. While we must receive Christ individually, the moment we do so we enter into a fellowship and become part of a body of like-minded people who have all trusted Jesus Christ, who himself becomes the strong bond which unites us all.

We share together in God's protection, guidance and teaching. We together enjoy the gift of his life, his Son and his Spirit. We are united as Christ's body, his temple (Eph. 2:20–22) and his bride (Rev. 19:7; Eph. 5:25–27), and are commissioned to be his witnesses. We are encouraged by the warmth of the fellowship, united in its love, strengthened by its power and stimulated by its enthusiasm. We progress in its vitality, overflow in its joy, become stable in its teaching and active in its advance.

There may be arguments and divisions along the way—differences in interpretations of the Scriptures and in minor doctrinal issues and practices—but beneath it all is the unifying life of the Lord Jesus. We are his children—all of us. We are in his family and, as part of his body, we are 'built together for a dwelling place of God in the Spirit' (Eph. 2:22).

SALVATION IS GREAT

God's salvation is great because of its Author (Heb. 2:3). Karl Barth has pointed out that the Apostles' Creed knows only one attribute of God: his almightiness. Barth says, 'The Father is almightiness and almightiness is the Father.'[8] God is might and in his limitless infinity and omnipotent freedom he is able to do anything he wills to do, but whatever he does will always be based upon his character of love, righteousness and holiness. Everything that this great God does is great. He speaks worlds into existence. He sustains 'all things by the word of His power' (Heb. 1:3). But when it comes to salvation, all else fades away. By restoring fallen man to himself, he reveals his great masterpiece in which he moves in majestic splendour and accomplishes his purposes for man. Salvation is great because it is an almighty God who accomplishes it.

It is also great because of the great price paid to procure it. The incarnation itself was enormously humiliating. Rejected when born, the One who is co-equal with the Father suffered at the hands of those whom he had created and whose lives he was sustaining even while they were persecuting him. Denied, forsaken, repudiated, accused, condemned and finally crucified—in him man's revolt against God was fully unveiled. Christ was rejected by man because his sinless life condemned their sinfulness. He was rejected by God because he became 'sin for us' (2 Cor. 5:21). Hanging between heaven and earth, he was cursed and crushed as a guilt-offering (Gal. 3:13; Isa. 53:10). Alone! What an awesome offering; what a fearful sacrifice; what 'precious blood' shed for our redemption (1 Peter 1:19)! How shall we escape if we neglect so great a salvation (Heb. 2:3)?

Salvation is great because of its executor, the Holy Spirit. He convicts the world of guilt in regard to sin and righteousness and judgement (John 16:8). He points man to Christ (John 15:26). He regenerates fallen man (John 3:3–6). By his indwelling, we belong to Christ (Rom. 8:9). He gives us the seal of divine ownership (Eph. 1:13). He testifies with our spirit that we are God's children (Rom. 8:16)! In fact, by his operation he makes possible Christ's work of salvation in the lives of believing sinners. He transfers to us the benefits of Calvary and Pentecost.

Salvation is great because of the blessings it brings. This salvation is not a man-reforming message of fallen flesh, but a life-transforming message of divine power. It is a message of forgiveness of sin's evil (1 John 1:9), reconciliation from sin's enmity (Rom. 5:10; 2 Cor. 5:19), cleansing from sin's defilement (2 Cor. 7:1; Ezek. 36:25) and liberation from sin's power (Rom. 6:14). The gospel 'is the power of God to salvation for everyone who believes'(Rom. 1:16); 'if anyone is in Christ, he is a new creation' (2 Cor. 5:17). We live in God and he in us (1 John 4:16). Truly God's salvation is great.

SALVATION IS SECURE

Christians in different traditions emphasize different aspects of biblical teaching, resulting at times in sharp disagreements. The security of the believer is one of those controversial topics. Fortunately, God does not say, 'Understand the truths concerning salvation, and you will be saved', but, 'Believe on the Lord Jesus Christ, and you will be saved' (Acts 16:31).

On this subject, the New Testament uses three significant words in relation to believers: 'election', 'foreknowledge' and 'predestination'. Two of these words are used together in Romans 8:29: 'For whom He foreknew, He also predestined to be conformed to the image of His Son.' Speaking of divine foreknowledge, Vine comments, 'Foreknowledge is one aspect of omniscience; it is implied in God's warnings, promises and predictions (see Acts 15:18). God's foreknowledge involves his electing grace but this does not preclude human will. He foreknows the exercise of faith which brings salvation.'[9] In his sovereignty, God gives to man responsibility.

There is, without a doubt, a mystery surrounding this doctrine and no one would claim to explain it adequately. Faith in Christ is the essential quality needed to experience salvation and this is where the emphasis must lie. In the desert, when poisonous snakes were biting the Israelites and many were dying, God told Moses to make a bronze snake and put it on a pole in the camp. Those who were bitten were to look at the bronze reptile and they would be saved from death (Num. 21:4–9). In explaining salvation, Jesus referred to this very story: 'And as Moses lifted up the serpent in the wilderness, even so must the Son of Man be lifted up, that whoever believes in Him should not perish but have eternal life' (John 3:14–15). How the poison was neutralized no one understood; but to those who believed and looked, it happened. Faith is also stressed in John 3:16: 'whoever believes in Him should not perish but have everlasting life.'

This emphasis on faith is clearly seen in the relevant passage in John's Gospel: 'My sheep hear [present tense: means 'keep on hearing'] My voice, and I know them, and they follow Me ['keep on following Me']. And I give ['keep on giving'] them eternal life, and they shall never perish; neither shall anyone snatch them out of My hand' (John 10:27–28). 'I keep on giving life to the sheep who keep on following me!' This statement is prefixed by the words 'you do not believe, because you are not of My sheep', implying, of course, that 'My sheep' have faith and are believing. They are the ones who are listening and following, who are constantly receiving life, who are being saved and will finally be saved.

'For I am persuaded', says Paul, 'that neither death nor life, nor angels nor principalities nor powers, nor things present nor things to come, nor height nor depth, nor any other created thing, shall be able to separate us from the love of God which is in Christ Jesus our Lord' (Rom. 8:38–39). What comfort and joy this great truth brings to the believer! God keeps us securely in his hand.

SALVATION IS ETERNAL

God assures us that salvation is 'everlasting' (Isa. 45:17). He says, 'My salvation will be forever' (Isa. 51:6) and through Paul he assures the Thessalonians that they 'shall always be with the Lord' (1 Thes. 4:17). He has become 'the author of eternal salvation to all who obey Him' (Heb. 5:9).

We are dealing with something which is vitally important, for if we can be eternally saved, we can also be eternally lost. These extremely solemn truths will affect our eternal destiny. Salvation is a matter for very serious contemplation because the consequences of neglecting its conditions and offer are eternal.

Those who know God as their Saviour are assured by the testimony of both the Word and the Spirit and are thrilled at the prospect of always being with him. Heaven is theirs—for ever.

The offer of salvation

IT IS FREE

'[T]he gift of God is eternal life in Christ Jesus our Lord' (Rom. 6:23). Salvation is not deserved, neither can it be bought or earned: 'For by grace you have been saved through faith, and that not of yourselves; it is the gift of God, not of works, lest anyone should boast' (Eph. 2:8–9). He saved us, not because of righteous things we have done, but 'according to His mercy' (Titus 3:5); 'all our righteousnesses are like filthy rags' (Isa. 64:6)—man's best efforts to obtain salvation end in failure.

Our own good works cannot form the grounds of acceptance with

God. Down through the centuries, man has insisted on trying to earn salvation by good deeds or by good character, but he cannot have it until he realizes that it is a gift which he must be willing to accept. Christ has paid the price for man's salvation and now man must swallow his pride and receive humbly from him what he alone can give.

IT IS UNIVERSAL
Biblical salvation is not the teaching of a bland universal salvation which has all men ultimately saved. However, God has declared that he is 'not willing that any should perish but that all should come to repentance' (2 Peter 3:9) and that he 'desires all men to be saved and to come to the knowledge of the truth' (1 Tim. 2:4).

God's love encompasses the world, and this is portrayed vividly in the best-known verse in the Bible: 'For God so loved the world that He gave His only begotten Son, that whoever believes in Him should not perish but have everlasting life' (John 3:16). We are told that Jesus 'gave Himself a ransom for all' (1 Tim. 2:6); 'He Himself is the propitiation for our sins, and not for ours only but also for the whole world' (1 John 2:2). He is 'The Lamb of God who takes away the sin of the world' (John 1:29). This certainly was a striking truth to reveal to Jews who knew only of sacrifices for Israelites. Christ's death was the grounds upon which God could deal with the whole race. God is no respecter of persons and he offers the benefits of Christ's death to everyone. The Scriptures present the atonement as able to procure and effective to secure salvation for all. Yet not all avail themselves of this eternal blessing and the sphere of its effective operation is limited to the church. The atonement is thus sufficient for all but is effective only for those who believe in Christ. As far as it lays the foundation for God's receptive dealing with all mankind, it is unlimited, but as far as its application is concerned, it is limited to those who actually believe in Christ. Potentially, Christ is the Saviour of all people (1 Tim. 1:15; 1 John 2:2); actually and effectively, he is the Saviour only of those who believe (1 Tim. 4:10). Faith is the touchstone. The door of salvation is open to all, for 'whoever calls on the name of the LORD shall be saved' (Acts 2:21). His free gift 'came to all men, resulting in justification of life' (Rom. 5:18).

Chapter 1

IT IS PERSONAL

It sounds very impersonal to speak of salvation for the world, but when we realize that salvation is for us, it is another matter altogether. I am part of God's world and when God says that he loves the world, it means that he loves me. For God so loved me that he gave his only begotten Son that, if I believe in him, I shall not perish but have eternal life. The Bible magnifies the worth of the individual and the dignity of human personality. God deals with everyone individually. Paul movingly expresses this in very intimate terms; he says, 'the Son of God ... loved me and gave Himself for me' (Gal. 2:20). Jesus looked over the sea of faces of the countless millions on earth and he saw me. He came to 'taste death for everyone', and that included me, even me (Heb. 2:9).

If Christ died for me, even though my friends may guide and help me, this salvation is a matter which I must personally settle with God. No one can deal with God for me, no priest or parent can answer to God on my behalf. I am on my own before God, and to God I must give account (Rom. 14:12).

IT IS A PERSON

Salvation is not something but Someone. It is not an it: it is a Person. It is not some intangible substance which will evaporate and leave us ashamed and embarrassed. It is not some vague and nebulous theory which eludes our understanding. It is Jesus Christ—a living, loving person: 'the riches of the glory of this mystery among the Gentiles: which is Christ in you, the hope of glory' (Col. 1:27). Christ lives 'in your hearts through faith' (Eph. 3:17). To save you, he must live in you! You must participate in the divine nature (2 Peter 1:4). He says, 'Behold, I stand at the door and knock. If anyone hears My voice and opens the door, I will come in to him and dine with him, and he with Me' (Rev. 3:20). There will be satisfying fellowship and blessed companionship all the way home to glory: 'But as many as received Him, to them He gave the right to become children of God, to those who believe in His name' (John 1:12). 'God has given us eternal life, and this life is in His Son. He who has the Son has life' (1 John 5:11–12). What authority we have—what joy! Life! Eternal life! This is ours in Christ as we dare to trust him to enter our meagre lives and enrich them immeasurably by his incomparable presence.

And this is only the beginning, for he who has begun a good work in us will 'complete it until the day of Jesus Christ' (Phil. 1:6) and will guard that which we have entrusted to him until he comes again and takes us to be with him for ever (2 Tim. 1:12).

The conditions of salvation

The conditions of salvation were clearly spelled out by Paul when he declared to both Jews and Greeks that they must turn to God in repentance and have faith in our Lord Jesus (Acts 20:21). Repentance and faith are the two essential qualities without which there can be no salvation.

REPENTANCE

The importance of repentance cannot be overestimated. It is given prominence in Scripture. It involves the whole person, intellectually, emotionally and volitionally.

Intellectually, it means a complete 'about face' in our thinking. The Greek word from which 'repentance' comes literally means 'a change of mind'. We must change our mind about effecting our own salvation. Man has always been determined to work out his own salvation, or at least to contribute to it. Repentance brings a change of mind so that he is prepared to relinquish that idea and accept God's free pardon. We must also change our minds about our goals. Our priorities will have to be reversed, our philosophies of life revolutionized. We must change our minds about sin. We cannot continue to pursue with relish our old ways and assume that God will unquestionably give us his salvation. The Bible knows no one who is saved yet unrepentant. You cannot enter heaven clutching your sins. We must change our minds about God. Whereas we had resisted God and refused to yield to his tender call, we now alter our attitudes and thoughts about him and respond to his love.

Emotionally, repentance means that we see ourselves as guilty of punishment. God convicts us of our sin and brings regret and sorrow for having committed it and for having acted so shamefully towards so loving a God. 'For godly sorrow produces repentance leading to salvation, not to be regretted; but the sorrow of the world produces death' (2 Cor. 7:10). Godly sorrow is not merely regret for the consequences of sin—for that which sin has brought upon me—but it is sorrow for the sin itself. The sorrow of Judas was remorse, while Peter's sorrow was repentance. Repentance has been described as 'true sorrow for sin, with a sincere effort to forsake it'. It is being 'sorry enough to quit'. Just how much emotion is necessary in repentance no one can say. It will probably vary a great deal from person to person, but a certain amount of heart movement normally accompanies all true repentance.

Volitionally, repentance means that we become willing to forsake our sins. 'Let the wicked forsake his way, And the unrighteous man his thoughts; Let him return to the LORD, And He will have mercy on him; And to our God, for He will abundantly pardon' (Isa. 55:7). 'He who covers his sins will not prosper, But whoever confesses and forsakes them will have mercy' (Prov. 28:13). The repentant attitude of heart must now be translated into action. The prodigal son said, '"I will arise and go to my father … " And he arose and came to his father' (Luke 15:18,20). The Holy Spirit helps us to repent by applying the Word to the mind and conscience, by touching the heart and by strengthening the will and the determination to turn from sin. Only as we turn to God will we be able to 'bear fruits worthy of repentance' (Matt. 3:8).

'God … now commands all men everywhere to repent' (Acts 17:30–31). Jesus began his ministry with the word 'Repent' (Matt. 4:17). Without repentance, there is no salvation.

FAITH

Without faith, repentance recedes into indifference or changes into morbid remorse. Paul declares that the gospel 'is the power of God to salvation for everyone who believes' and that the 'just shall live by faith' (Rom. 1:16–17). He says that it is 'by grace you have been saved through faith' (Eph. 2:8). Therefore, the promise comes by 'faith that it might be according to grace' (Rom. 4:16); 'without faith it is impossible to please Him' (Heb. 11:6). Faith is therefore absolutely essential.

What is saving faith? It is not natural faith. Natural faith is the normal day-to-day trust in the many areas of life. I switch on the light, not because I understand electricity, but because I believe that it provides a means of lighting my room. I put the key into the lock on my car door because I believe that it will unlock the door. The agreement with accepted norms or doctrines is not saving faith.

It is not temporal faith, such as God answering prayer for a sick child to get better or for a husband to get a job. These answers are no proof of sonship. Why, Jesus even answered the prayer of demons on one occasion. They begged Jesus, 'If You cast us out, permit us to go away into the herd of swine.' And he replied, 'Go' (Matt. 8:31–32).

It is not merely knowledge. A Christian worker was once explaining the gospel to a man but was stopped when this man related the gospel back to him with many biblical quotations. Unfortunately, he was drunk. He knew all about the gospel but it had no effect upon him.

It is not faith in a book, even if that book is the Bible. It is not faith in a creed, however many hundreds of years it may have stood. It is not faith in an institution, even if the institution is the church. It is not even faith in the being of God. 'Even the demons believe—and tremble!' (James 2:19).

Saving faith is trusting Christ alone for salvation. It is the sure confidence that Christ died for my sins, that he loved me and gave himself for me. It is the act of personal heart trust by which sinners commit themselves to God and accept as their own the salvation which God freely offers them in Christ.

It is the act of the penitent only, aided by the Spirit and resting upon Christ. A verse in the Amplified Bible is illuminating: 'For with the heart a person believes (adheres to, trusts in, and relies on Christ) and so is justified' (Rom. 10:10).

To have faith we must have something in which to believe. A certain amount of intellectual faith must therefore precede saving faith. We must know that there is a God to whom we must give account, that we are sinners deserving punishment, that Jesus died as our substitute and that he offers us eternal life; 'faith comes by hearing, and hearing by the word of God' (Rom. 10:17).

But giving only intellectual assent to these truths will never bring us salvation. We must trust them to be effective in our lives, and trust Christ alone to save us. It is all very well knowing and believing that if we walk across a bridge we will get to the other side, but if we do not put our faith into action and step out over the bridge, we will never get there. Similarly, we can know that Jesus is the Son of God and the Saviour of the world; we can know that he can and will save us if we trust him; but if we do not actually trust him, we will be lost.

Let us exercise faith for our sins to be forgiven (1 John 1:9) and to receive him as our indwelling Saviour and Lord (John 1:12), in doing so receiving from him eternal life (John 3:16).

Forsaking

All

I

Trust

Him

Notes

1 **Sinclair B. Ferguson, David F. Wright, J. I. Packer** (eds.), *New Dictionary of Theology* (Leicester: IVP, 1988), p. 610.

2 **Alan Cairns** (ed.), *Dictionary of Theological Terms* (Belfast: Ambassadors, 1998), p. 324.

3 **Merrill C. Tenney** (ed.), *Zondervan's Pictorial Bible Dictionary* (Grand Rapids, MI: Zondervan, 1963), p. 744.

4 **G. Henderson,** *The Salvation of God* (Edinburgh: McCall Barbour, 1960), p. 12.

5 **W. T. Purkiser** (ed.), *God, Man and Salvation* (Kansas City, MO: Beacon Hill, 1977), p. 367.

6 **B. S. Easton** in **J. Orr** (ed.), *International Standard Bible Encyclopedia*, vol. iv (1939; 1976, Grand Rapids, MI: Eerdmans), p. 2665.

7 **J. D. Douglas** (ed.), *The New Bible Dictionary* (London: IVP, 1962), p. 1127.

8 **Karl Barth,** *Dogmatics in Outline* (London: SCM, 1949), p. 46.

9 **W. E. Vine,** *Expository Dictionary of New Testament Words* (London: Oliphants, 1939), p. 119.

Repentance: forsaking sin with godly sorrow

Definitions of repentance

- 'Repentance unto life is a saving grace, whereby a sinner—out of a true sense of his sin and apprehension of the mercy of God in Christ—doth with grief and hatred of his sin, turn from it unto God, with full purpose of, and endeavour after, new obedience' (*Westminster Shorter Catechism*).[1]
- 'Repentance is a grace of God's Spirit whereby a sinner is inwardly humbled and visibly transformed' (Thomas Watson).[2]
- 'Sorrow and contrition with respect to sin are included in the Bible idea of repentance, but these follow and are consequent upon the sinner's change of mind with respect to it' (Kenneth S. Wuest).[3]
- 'Repentance may be defined as that change wrought in the conscious life of the sinner by which he turns away from sin' (Louis Berkhof).[4]
- 'Repentance involves a change of mind towards self, which is always too highly regarded; towards sin, which is too lightly regarded; and towards God, whose sovereignty is disregarded' (Frank Boyd).[5]
- 'Repentance is godly sorrow for sin that leads to forsaking and renouncing sin and turning to Christ for forgiveness of sin and salvation from sin. In real repentance the sinner's heart is broken because of his sin and that leads to separation from the sin. Repentance involves the whole personality' (Wesley L. Duewel).[6]
- 'Repentance means a change of mind that leads to a change of life-style' (Sinclair Ferguson).[7]
- 'Repentance is not only a heart broken for sin but from sin also. We must forsake what we would have God remit' (William Evans).[8]
- 'Repentance is a heartfelt sorrow for sin, a renouncing of it, and a sincere commitment to forsake it and walk in obedience to Christ' (Wayne Grudem).[9]

The importance of repentance

A correct biblical understanding of the doctrine of sin is essential for the understanding of salvation. If man's sin were to be seen merely as harmless faults and imperfections which could somehow be excused, there would be no need for the atoning sacrifices of the Old Testament, which all pointed to and culminated in the moment when God's Lamb died on our behalf 'to put away sin by the sacrifice of Himself' (Heb. 9:26). God's character is holy and sin cannot stand in his presence. His righteousness must condemn sin or his character would be compromised.

Sin is therefore an evil which separates God from man but, just as the righteousness of God demands judgement on sin, so the love of God provides the Substitute for sin. God projected himself into the human race in the person of his Son. 'God was in Christ reconciling the world to Himself' (2 Cor. 5:19). Christ identified himself with our sin and took the punishment for that sin. Salvation originates in and is executed by God, and it is salvation by substitution. Having put away sin, he now calls us to repent of that sin and to turn to him in humility and contrition: 'God ... now commands all men everywhere to repent' (Acts 17:30).

Repentance is often the missing note in today's easy presentation of the gospel. The positive aspects of salvation are emphasized and offered: 'Come to Jesus and you will have peace, joy, happiness and rest.' Everybody wants peace, joy, happiness and rest! There is no offence there! This is good psychology, but it does not take sin into account! Without repentance—turning away from sin—these wonderful qualities will not be experienced. There is no salvation apart from repentance. The positive can only be experienced if the negative is acknowledged and the sin forsaken. A holy God does not co-exist with persistent sin in the heart. For sin to be removed, it must be acknowledged, confessed and forsaken. 'He who covers his sins will not prosper, But whoever confesses and forsakes them will have mercy' (Prov. 28:13). There must be repentance and a forsaking of sin. God is then able to forgive and cleanse that sin away. The blood covers that which we uncover.

Notice the importance that is placed upon repentance in the Scriptures. In numerous places the Old Testament prophets called upon the nation to repent. Repentance is in evidence very frequently in the psalms. In the New Testament we find the following:

- John the Baptist: 'Repent, for the kingdom of heaven is at hand!' (Matt. 3:2); 'And he went into all the region around the Jordan, preaching a baptism of repentance for the remission of sins' (Luke 3:3).
- Jesus Christ: 'The time is fulfilled, and the kingdom of God is at hand. Repent, and believe in the gospel' (Mark 1:15).
- Christ's disciples: 'So they went out and preached that people should repent' (Mark 6:12).
- Peter at Pentecost: 'Repent, and let every one of you be baptized in the name of Jesus Christ for the remission of sins' (Acts 2:38).
- Peter again: 'Repent therefore and be converted, that your sins may be blotted out, so that times of refreshing may come from the presence of the Lord' (Acts 3:19).
- Peter to Simon the sorcerer: 'Repent therefore of this your wickedness, and pray God if perhaps the thought of your heart may be forgiven you' (Acts 8:22).
- Parable of the lost sheep: 'likewise there will be more joy in heaven over one sinner who repents than over ninety-nine just persons' (Luke 15:7).
- Parable of the lost coin: 'Likewise, I say to you, there is joy in the presence of the angels of God over one sinner who repents' (Luke 15:10).
- Parable of the prodigal son: 'And the son said to him, "Father I have sinned … " But the father said … "this my son was dead and is alive again; he was lost and is found"' (Luke 15:21–24).
- Christ's commission: 'repentance and remission of sins should be preached in His name to all nations' (Luke 24:47).
- Response to Peter's defence of his ministry among the Gentiles: 'Then God has also granted to the Gentiles repentance to life' (Acts 11:18).
- Paul in Athens: 'God … now commands all men everywhere to repent' (Acts 17:30).
- Paul to the Ephesian elders: 'testifying to Jews, and also to Greeks, repentance toward God and faith toward our Lord Jesus Christ' (Acts 20:21).

- Paul's calling and charge: 'to make you a minister and a witness … to open their eyes, in order to turn them from darkness to light, and from the power of Satan to God, that they may receive forgiveness of sins' (Acts 26:16,18).
- Paul before Agrippa: '[I] declared first to those in Damascus and in Jerusalem, and throughout all the region of Judea, and then to the Gentiles, that they should repent, turn to God, and do works befitting repentance' (Acts 26:20).
- The writer to the Hebrews: 'let us go on to perfection, not laying again the foundation of repentance from dead works and of faith toward God' (Heb. 6:1).
- Peter: 'The Lord is not slack concerning His promise, as some count slackness, but is longsuffering toward us, not willing that any should perish but that all should come to repentance' (2 Peter 3:9).
- Repentance produced by the Word of God: the servant of the Lord must in humility be 'correcting those who are in opposition, if God perhaps will grant them repentance, so that they may know the truth' (2 Tim. 2:25).
- The churches in Revelation 2–3: five of the seven churches to which Christ wrote had deviated from the purity of the gospel in teaching and practice. Did he exhort them to show more love, to discuss their various doctrinal differences, to do good works, to be kind to one another? No! He stated sternly that they should 'Repent' (2:5,16,22; 3:3). That was the way back to God!
- John the Baptist, Christ and his disciples all began their ministries with the word 'Repent'. This indicates the absolute necessity of repentance.

Repentance is necessary for forgiveness
- 'Repent … for the remission of [your] sins' (Acts 2:38).
- 'Repent … that your sins may be blotted out' (Acts 3:19).
- ' … unless you repent you will all likewise perish' (Luke 13:3,5).
- 'Let the wicked forsake his way, And the unrighteous man his thoughts; Let him return to the LORD, And He will have mercy on him; And to our God, For He will abundantly pardon' (Isa. 55:7).

- ' ... if My people who are called by My name will humble themselves, and pray and seek My face, and turn from their wicked ways, then I will hear from heaven, and will forgive their sin and heal their land' (2 Chron. 7:14).

Forgiveness is that one great word which characterizes the Christian religion. An almighty God sovereignly forgives people who approach him in sincerity and humility. They are brought to a state of conviction of their sinful condition by the Holy Spirit and cry to God for forgiveness on the basis of the substitutionary offering for sin made by Jesus Christ. As they reach up in faith they are forgiven by a merciful God who has accepted Christ's offering on their behalf. That begins their Christian journey. Without that momentous event of repentance and faith they are outside grace and are under the condemnation of God (Acts 20:21). Christ's great sacrifice at Calvary is the heart and kernel of the Christian faith. It is here that God meets man in mercy and love, and it is here that man is restored to a relationship of peace with his heavenly Father. Forgiveness is only experienced when we repent of our sins and trust Christ to save us.

False repentance

To discover what true repentance is, we must first find out what it is not, for people may delude themselves with a counterfeit repentance. Some folk respond in a way which to them seems to be repentance but which is actually only a faint resemblance of it. Persuading themselves that they have already repented, they sleep contentedly on a pillow of false security.

LEGAL REPENTANCE

Some hear the gospel, accept its truth and their consciences are awakened and alarmed. They need to pacify their guilty consciences, satisfy divine justice and gain some hope of eternal life. They conclude that, because they have experienced bitter anguish as they contemplated their sin, they have, as far as they can assess, experienced some measure of repentance. The only way for them now, it would seem, is to increase their earnestness, pray that God will have mercy upon them and hope that in his electing purposes they might be the eventual recipients of divine favour.

The fear of God's wrath leads to reformation of life but sadly to an experience which falls short of salvation. They remain religious, devout and outwardly devoted to the proclamation of the gospel. They seem to be part of the worshipping body of believers but they have not exercised saving faith. They are with the body of believers, but not of them. Their lives are exemplary: they are religious, kind and live good lives. Looking on, one would say that they were true Christians, yet their service is hard, cold, legal and without the joy of those who have experienced the forgiveness of God and the indwelling life of Christ. They are resting on false foundations, for although they might have changed outwardly, they have never trusted savingly. They have religion but not reality; they are serious but not saved.

MERITORIOUS REPENTANCE

Firstly, repentance is not doing good works, although some seem to think that by doing good they earn favour with God. They help, they are involved in all sorts of good causes, they look after people, they run errands for the needy; and they suppose that God accepts and is pleased with all these decent and commendable deeds. They think that their good actions outweigh their bad ones and that they will be accepted by God. After all, they are following good decisions and are not indulging in repulsive behaviour which they have left far behind in their quest for God's favour. They have not realized that 'all our righteousnesses are like filthy rags' (Isa. 64:6). We have no goodness in ourselves, but only as Christ lives his life through us are good deeds the evidence of his righteousness in us.

Secondly, some attempt to gain God's mercy by afflicting themselves. This could even at times take the form of physical affliction. They deny themselves all sorts of things and think that that kind of self-denial is a form of repentance and is therefore acceptable to God. Self-denial as a form of merit or acceptance with God is thought to bring them into a saving relationship with God. They would never turn to open sin and objectionable actions, so God would surely never turn them away! They have a reputation to live up to and the community regards them as decent people who lead good lives. They surely expect to receive God's mercy and salvation when they come to the end of this life. Sadly, they are deceived.

REFORMATION

People may make decisions and vows yet not be penitent. They may turn their lives around yet not increase in godliness. 'They return, but not to the Most High' (Hosea 7:16). Isaiah saw this possible loophole and said,

Let the wicked forsake his way,
And the unrighteous man his thoughts;
Let him return to the LORD,
And He will have mercy on him;
And to our God,
For He will abundantly pardon
(Isa. 55:7).

We are required not merely to forsake sin but to return to God and there find pardon! Forsaking sin may be accomplished by strength of will; it brings about a change in behaviour but it does not bring about an inward transformation, for the person has not returned to God and consequently has not had a divine encounter. Paul declared that sinners 'should repent, turn to God, and do works befitting repentance' (Acts 26:20). The Thessalonians 'turned to God from idols to serve the living and true God' (1 Thes. 1:9). They did not merely turn away from idols but they turned to God, and they followed this up by serving him. Their whole lives were on a new track.

TEMPORARY REPENTANCE

Having been moved by an earnest conversation, a fervent sermon, a sickness or death in the family or the impact of a beautiful, Christ-centred life, some recognize their need of God and turn to him in that need. They vow that they will reform their ways, and will, from this moment on, follow the Lord. It is but short lived, for when the emotion of the event subsides, their seeming conversion evaporates and they return to their old ways. Jesus speaks of this kind of person in the parable of the sower and the seed in Mark 4. Some of the seed fell on stony ground, sprang up but did not last long, a picture of those who 'have no root in themselves, and so endure only for a time' (v. 17). Their response to the gospel is a temporary affair and the enjoyment of their former ways soon pulls them back.

REMORSEFUL REPENTANCE

Many repent because of the consequences of sin. Thieves may be sorry when they are caught, not because they have stolen, but because they will have to pay the penalty for stealing. They are sorry for what their sin has brought upon them. Hypocrites grieve over the bitter consequences of their sin.

Pharaoh was more sorry about the river of blood, the frogs and the hail than about his sin. He said, 'I have sinned this time. The Lord is righteous, and my people and I are wicked'; yet when the thunderings and the hail ceased, he hardened his heart (Exod. 9:27,34).

Similarly, when Balaam saw the Angel of the Lord standing in the way with a drawn sword in his hand, he said, 'I have sinned', but he continued on his rebellious way (Num. 22:34). When the judgements of God fly into the conscience, we repent in some measure, yet it is often not enough to bring us to faith in God.

People are exposed and they fear the sting of public disapproval. The opinions of their families and friends count a great deal and this brings them to a place of seeming contrition and repentance. They would even try to put right the wrongs that they have done and which are now exposed. So they 'repent'.

There is a difference between repentance and remorse. Peter repented and wept bitterly. His was true repentance, for he returned to the Lord and became a mighty champion of the faith. In contrast, Judas was filled with remorse and horror at what he had done. He actually made restitution and gave back the thirty pieces of silver. This, however, was not true repentance but remorse. He had been exposed. Everyone knew him now for what he was and the pain was too heavy to bear. He tragically ended his own life.

TEARFUL REPENTANCE

Sometimes there are tears, but not all tears are evidence of true repentance. Some weep when they hear a powerful sermon, but it is like an April shower—soon over! Some pour out tears because they have been discovered in their sin and the pain of exposure is too much. Some weep because of those whom they have hurt and offended during their time away from God. Some weep because of the dreadful state that they are in and the crimes they have committed through the ravages of sin. Some weep because of their sin, yet they are not prepared to forsake that sin and consequently they never get any further in their quest for God. Some weep because they never get to the place of finding forgiveness, as they never exercise faith.

Paul exhorts such people to be 'sorry in a godly manner ... [for] the sorrow of the world produces death' (2 Cor. 7:9). There are those who sorrow in a manner which brings them no benefit, for it does not lead them to true repentance and faith.

DEATHBED REPENTANCE

Fearing the consequences of God's terrible judgement, and realizing that they are now at the end of life without needing to live out this Christian experience before their acquaintances, many turn to God in their last moments. Some are sincere, but others have no intention of changing their ways should they recover from their illnesses. They want an insurance policy from hell in their last moments.

I once heard the revivalist Duncan Campbell tell of his experience in the trenches of the First World War. They were to 'go over the top' the next day and they knew that many of them would be killed in the attack. He was summoned by around six of his fellow soldiers who knew him as a religious fellow. They wanted to know how to trust God in the face of this terrible prospect. He explained the gospel to them and they, in seeming utter sincerity, trusted Christ to save them. He said that he had rarely seen such sincerity anywhere. The battle was fought and they all survived; yet when he suggested to them that they return thanks to God, they laughed him to scorn and ridiculed his religious convictions. It was deathbed repentance, and it was worthless. They were as unsaved as they had ever been, with no intentions of following the Lord.

PARTIAL REPENTANCE

Many feel the weight of their wrongdoing and know that the only way to gain God's favour is to repent. Yet they are not prepared to leave everything for Christ's sake. We read that Israel's '"treacherous sister Judah has not turned to Me with her whole heart, but in pretense," says the LORD' (Jer. 3:10). People break off a sin here and another there, hoping that this gradual betterment will appease the Almighty and gain them favour. They read the Bible on occasions and they pray at times. They respond appropriately to stern warnings of gospel truths and rid themselves of yet other sins. This is hopeless.

What is needed is a total capitulation, an earnest confession, a relinquishment of all that which is displeasing to God, a turning from the old ways and a turning to the Lord who will forgive them and will indwell their redeemed souls. This total commitment they are not prepared to give, so they remain outside divine grace in semi-light. They have just enough religion to make themselves miserable, for they know that when they indulge in questionable things they are condemned within their own hearts, and when they mingle with the saints of God they are again condemned because they know that they should be with them in glad consecration but are not. Their sad state is unenviable and can but lead to the terrible judgements of a holy and righteous God.

True repentance

REVELATION

In the prodigal's repentance, the first aspect was that 'he came to himself' (Luke 15:17). He became conscious of his waywardness. There was insight and an inward understanding of his condition.

In his great prayer, Solomon speaks of the Israelites sinning and being taken captive, 'yet when they come to themselves … and repent … saying, "We have sinned" … and when they return to You with all their heart … then hear in heaven Your dwelling place their prayer … and forgive Your people' (1 Kings 8:47–50). They, too, needed first to 'come to themselves'.

Job says, 'But now my eye sees You. Therefore I abhor myself And repent in dust and ashes' (Job 42:5–6). The sight of a holy God brought hatred of his condition.

It was the vision of the Lord which brought repentance to the prophet Isaiah. There was revelation before repentance. 'In the year that King Uzziah died, I saw the Lord ... So I said, "Woe is me, for I am undone! Because I am a man of unclean lips"' (Isa. 6:1,5).

It was when Nathan the prophet pointed out to David his sin that the bitter cry of repentance in Psalm 51 was wrenched from his heart.

When Jesus turned and looked at Peter, that look exposed his denial and melted his heart, and he went out and wept bitterly (Luke 22:61–62).

When Peter preached at Pentecost, 'they were cut to the heart, and said to Peter and the rest of the apostles, "Men and brethren, what shall we do?"' (Acts 2:37).

There is a moment when we come face to face with God and it brings about a mighty humbling, a confession, a repudiation of evil, a turning to God in sincerity and faith: a true repentance.

REALIZATION

'I will be in anguish over my sin' (Ps. 38:18); 'then they will look on Me whom they pierced ... they will mourn' (Zech. 12:10). When we realize that we truly are sinners before a holy God, that there is no good in us, that there is no hope for us, that we are under God's righteous condemnation that we have infringed God's law and abused his love, then we eat the bitter bread of sorrow in holy agony. There will be sorrow that we did not repent sooner, that the garrisons of our hearts were closed to the One who loved us and died for us. There is an inevitable sorrow of heart. In Scripture it is called a breaking of the heart:

The sacrifices of God are a broken spirit,
A broken and a contrite heart—
These, O God, You will not despise
(Ps. 51:17).

The fact that we have grieved God should break our hearts. Not all have the same degree of sorrow and there is no measure by which we can say that the sorrow expressed is sufficient. Some have sharper pangs than others, but all who come will know that they have offended their loving heavenly Father, and this brings grief: grief strong enough to make us let go of the offending sins. We will be sorry enough to quit!

CONFESSION

The prodigal confessed his sin before his father charged him with it. He said, 'Father, I have sinned against heaven and in your sight' (Luke 15:21). David said, 'my iniquities have gone over my head; like a heavy burden they are too heavy for me' (Ps. 38:4). The thief on the cross made a sincere confession of his sin: referring to his sin and punishment on the cross he said, 'We indeed [have been condemned] justly', to which Christ replied, 'today you will be with Me in Paradise' (Luke 23:41,43).

These voluntary confessions are deeply sincere. True confession leaves a heart-wounding impression on the soul. It does not simply slip off the tongue and mean nothing to the life. It is easy to say 'I am a poor sinner and I have offended God and many others' without meaning a thing. True confession costs, for we have sinned against God! Our hearts should go along with our confession. Sometimes we need to acknowledge particular sins.

The confessions of some are excuses rather than confessions. God asked Adam, 'Have you eaten from the tree of which I commanded you that you should not eat?' Adam replied, 'The woman whom You gave to be with me, she gave me of the tree, and I ate' (Gen. 3:11–12). Although he sinned, Adam blamed God and the woman! When Samuel confronted King Saul about his disobedience, Saul replied, 'I have sinned … because I feared the people' (1 Sam. 15:24). The people were to blame, not him! Instead of having tears to lament their sin, such people have arguments to defend it.

Confession must always be made to God, against whom we have sinned. David said, 'Against You, You only, have I sinned, and done this evil in Your sight' (Ps. 51:4). Sometimes it is necessary to confess to other people as well. If, for instance, you have sinned against the church, then not only must you confess to God, but you must also confess to the church and ask their forgiveness. If, however, you have sinned against one or two people, then the confession must be made to God and to those one or two people for their forgiveness as well. It is not necessary then to make a public confession to the church, for that merely spreads distaste and unrest, and the sordid details would be offensive or polluting to hear. If you have sinned against one person, it is necessary to confess to God and to that one person as well, but not to the whole group.

RENUNCIATION

True confession leads to forsaking of sins. Some confess yet return to their sins and continue in them. That is not true confession. The Scriptures speak of the dog returning to his own vomit, and the sow, having washed, to her wallowing in the mire (2 Peter 2:22). True confession leads, not to hiding our sins or returning to them, but to forsaking them.

This brings us to the heart of the meaning of repentance. The Greek words *metanoia* (used twenty-three times) and *metanoeo* (used thirty-four times) are the New Testament's chief expressions of repentance. Both mean a change of mind or purpose. This repentance is to be understood as a change of mind that leads to a change of lifestyle. It is not merely a sense of regret; it is an entire reversal of conduct, a lifelong change of mindset, as we forsake sin and submit to God. It is more than forgiveness; it means a transformed life. It is a renunciation of sin and sinful practices: 'godly sorrow produces repentance leading to salvation' (2 Cor. 7:10). It is an inner change of one's whole selfhood. As a result of true regret and sorrow for sin, the whole being is changed from following sin to following Christ.

'Repent and turn to God,' said Paul (see Acts 26:20). Turning from our own way to God's way *is* repentance. It is impossible to transfer our trust from self to Christ without repentance because that is precisely what repentance is. To be saved we must believe, but we cannot truly believe without repenting any more than we can travel from A to B without leaving A. So repentance, conversion and faith in Christ merge in God's great act of salvation. Repentance is a turning, a change of allegiance, placing faith in and following a new Master.

The Westminster Confession of Faith says this:

By it [repentance] a sinner, out of the sight and sense not only of the danger, but also of the filthiness and odiousness of his sins, as contrary to the holy nature, and righteous law of God; and upon the apprehension of His mercy in Christ to such as are penitent, so grieves for, and hates his sins, as to turn from them all unto God, purposing and endeavouring to walk with Him in all the ways of His commandments.[10]

A missionary friend in Africa was once preaching on this subject. The Zulu word for 'repent' is *pendukani*. In his message he called out three times, 'pendukani!' But *pendukani* also means to turn around, so there, under the tree, all the congregation turned around, turning their backs on him. He called them back and told them that they had just given him a good illustration, for that is what repentance really means—to turn around and to go in an entirely new direction.

INCLUSION

Repentance includes the whole personality. It affects the intellect, the emotions and the will.

THE SINNER'S MIND IS INVOLVED

Sinners change their minds about being able to effect their own salvation, realizing that this is impossible; sinners change their minds about sin and about God. Their intellects are illumined by the Holy Spirit and they begin to understand the holiness of God (Isa. 6), the rebellion of their sin (Rom. 1:32), the defilement of their sin (Job 42:6) and their personal guilt for their sin (Luke 15:18). They know how helpless they are apart from the mercy of God. Their understanding of things changes.

The son who was asked to work in his father's vineyard first said, 'I will not', but 'afterward he regretted it and went' (Matt. 21:29). His mind sprang into action and he changed his decision to his great benefit.

THE SINNER'S EMOTIONS ARE INVOLVED

A changed emotional experience is part of true repentance. Jesus told the story of the tax collector who stood afar off and 'would not so much as raise his eyes to heaven, but beat his breast, saying, "God be merciful to me a sinner!"' (Luke 18:13). The emotions of sinners can move them powerfully to seek deliverance from sin: 'When I kept silent, my bones grew old through my groaning all the day long ... I acknowledged my sin to You' (Ps. 32:3,5); 'godly sorrow produces repentance leading to salvation' (2 Cor. 7:10). Sinners realize how obnoxious their sin is to God and they recoil from it; they are sorry for it, and that leads them on to salvation.

THE SINNER'S WILL IS INVOLVED

The other elements of repentance are incomplete without this; the volitional element is essential. Weeping over your sin cannot replace your abandoning it and turning to God for his mercy. The understanding of the condition, the emotional experience of the consciousness of sin, must lead to an actual turning from sin to God for salvation from that sin. Not only did the prodigal decide to return to his father, but he also got up and actually went to his father. His intellectual grasp of the situation and his emotional frustration led to action. He rose and went to his father, and there found mercy and forgiveness.

RESTITUTION

Restitution is a part of repentance. A truly repentant person will attempt to make restitution as far as possible. We are to restore anything that we have stolen or make amends by compensation for loss, damage or injury. This principle is given in Exodus 22:1–6; Leviticus 6:2–5; and Numbers 5:6–8.

Zacchaeus said to Jesus, 'if I have taken anything from anyone by false accusation, I restore fourfold' (Luke 19:8). He who has injured his neighbour but refuses, though he has the ability, to make restitution is unrighteous. To pretend to have turned from iniquity with bitter repentance yet to enjoy the fruits of it is false. Things must be restored and compensations made if at all possible.

Sometimes the returning of stolen goods or the restoring of relationships gives a wonderful opportunity for testimony, even though the stealing may have taken place in the distant past or the goods not have been of great value, or even though the relationships might have healed somewhat over the years.

There are, of course, things which can never be restored, such as lost purity or lost lives. We can but leave these in God's hands.

APPROPRIATION

Faith is the God-ordained condition of salvation: 'without faith it is impossible to please Him' (Heb. 11:6). Paul preached 'repentance toward God and faith toward our Lord Jesus Christ' (Acts 20:21). Repentance without faith will only result in a morbid life of sorrow and grief. True repentance must be accompanied by faith to be effective and life-transforming.

Does repentance precede or follow the exercise of faith? Unless sinners understand and believe their lost condition without Christ, they will see no need of repentance. But the belief which thus produces penitence is not necessarily the faith which saves or justifies them.

The jailor at Philippi trembled and was afraid when he cried out, 'what must I do to be saved?' Paul and Silas said, 'Believe on the Lord Jesus Christ, and you will be saved' (Acts 16:30–31). He understood and had faith enough to believe that he was lost, but he needed to exercise saving faith in order for his repentance to be effective for the saving of his soul. Jesus preached, 'Repent, and believe in the gospel' (Mark 1:15).

As the Spirit works in the hearts of those who are seeking God, there is a repentance and an exercise of faith which is simultaneous. Repentance and saving faith are inseparable. They are part of each other. Every true believer is at the same time a true penitent, and every true penitent is a true believer. Nothing less produces a transformed life. There must be faith in the God who, for Christ's sake, accepts the repentance brought about by the working of the Holy Spirit.

FRUIT

John the Baptist exhorted the Pharisees and Sadducees to 'bear fruits worthy of repentance' (Matt. 3:8; Luke 3:8). Paul exclaimed that all 'should repent, turn to God, and do works befitting repentance' (Acts

26:20). Christlike living is the evidence of justification. Good works done and seen by all are the evidence of genuine faith. That which is within the heart is recognized as true when it is seen in the life. Fruit is life given away and appreciated by those who eat its tender morsels and who then acknowledge its true origin and genuine character. Without fruit, repentance is not genuine and neither has the soul had a saving encounter with the Almighty: 'faith by itself, if it does not have works, is dead' (James 2:17).

The motivation for repentance

IT IS GOD'S WILL
'The Lord is ... not willing that any should perish but that all should come to repentance' (2 Peter 3:9). Every day that comes to us is a gift of mercy and an opportunity to repent. Time is always to be regarded as an opportunity. 'God has committed them all to disobedience, that He might have mercy on all' (Rom. 11:32); he 'desires all men to be saved and to come to the knowledge of the truth' (1 Tim. 2:4). '"Do I have any pleasure at all that the wicked should die?" says the Lord GOD, "and not that he should turn from his ways and live?"' (Ezek. 18:23). God wills that all should come to repentance.

IT IS GOD'S COMMAND
'God ... now commands all men everywhere to repent, because He has appointed a day on which He will judge the world in righteousness' (Acts 17:30–31). Here on Mars Hill, Paul declared that God would judge the world and that his hearers' responsibility to prepare for that event was to repent. They were to consider their positions, change their minds and get away from the false conceptions which had led them to worship an 'Unknown God' (v. 23). So God's Word comes clearly to us today to leave our old pursuits, our old gods, and turn wholeheartedly to God.

IT IS GOD'S GIFT
'... if God perhaps will grant them repentance, so that they may know the

truth' (2 Tim. 2:25); 'Him God has exalted to His right hand to be Prince and Savior, to give repentance to Israel and forgiveness of sins' (Acts 5:31); 'God has also granted to the Gentiles repentance to life' (Acts 11:18). The gift of repentance is connected, therefore, with knowing the truth, the forgiveness of sins and the receiving of eternal life. Repentance is a divine gift so inseparably connected to salvation as to be an essential part of it. If it is a gift, how then can we be blamed for not being repentant? We are commanded to repent and when we feel our inability to do so, we are thrown upon God and are then able to cry to him to perform this work of grace in our hearts.

IT IS GOD-DIRECTED
Paul wrote that 'the goodness of God leads you to repentance' (Rom. 2:4). In his love, God directs us through a maze of circumstances, remarks, sermons, incidents and events which speak to us of his holiness and our sinfulness. We journey on, not knowing that God is engineering all these things in order that he may bring us to see ourselves in the light of eternity and then cry to him for mercy as we repent of our sins. In his goodness, he leads us all the way there.

IT IS GOD-INDUCED
'For godly sorrow produces repentance leading to salvation, not to be regretted; but the sorrow of the world produces death' (2 Cor. 7:9). Paul wrote a letter which made the Corinthian believers sorry (v. 8), but that sorrow 'led to repentance'. His rebukes and exhortations turned their hearts to seek God 'in a godly manner'. They responded to the rebukes from the preacher and sought God in repentance.

IT IS GOD-INSPIRED
It is impossible truly to repent without the operation of the Holy Spirit. When Peter recounted his ministry to the Gentiles, he said that 'the Holy Spirit fell upon them'; his hearers responded by saying, 'Then God has also granted to the Gentiles repentance to life' (Acts 11:15,18). The Holy Spirit drew the Gentiles to the Lord in whom they exercised faith for salvation when they repented.

IT IS PRODUCED BY GOSPEL PREACHING

Peter preached at Pentecost and 'when they [the people] heard this, they were cut to the heart, and said to Peter and the rest of the apostles, "Men and brethren, what shall we do?" Then Peter said to them, "Repent ... "' (Acts 2:37–38). The gospel which calls for repentance produces it. The gospel is the instrument which God uses to bring about the repentance he demands. This gospel must be preached in the power of the Holy Spirit, for Paul says, 'our gospel did not come to you in word only, but also in power, and in the Holy Spirit and in much assurance ... [Y]ou turned to God from idols to serve the living and true God' (1 Thes. 1:5,9).

IT IS PRODUCED BY CHASTISEMENT

'As many as I love, I rebuke and chasten. Therefore be zealous and repent' (Rev. 3:19); 'whom the LORD loves He chastens' (Heb. 12:6). The chastenings of the Lord are sometimes used to bring his wandering children back to repentance. God in mercy allows tragedies to occur to stop people in their tracks and cause them to take stock of their situations and return to the Lord.

IT IS PRODUCED BY REPROOF

'And a servant of the Lord must ... be gentle ... in humility correcting those who are in opposition, if God perhaps will grant them repentance' (2 Tim. 2:24–25). God sometimes uses the loving Christian reproof of a brother or sister to bring us back to God.

The consequences of repentance

JOY IN HEAVEN

The stories in Luke 15 tell of the lost sheep, the lost coin and the lost son, and all speak of the joy which was experienced when these were found: '"Rejoice with me, for I have found my sheep which was lost!" ... Likewise, I say to you, there is joy in the presence of the angels of God over one sinner who repents' (vv. 6,10). Joy in heaven! The angels rejoicing! The heart of God made glad! Why? Because one sinner has repented and turned back to God.

FORGIVENESS

'Repent therefore and be converted, that your sins may be blotted out' (Acts 3:19). Repentance does not qualify anyone for a pardon but it is a condition of one. We cannot earn forgiveness, we do not deserve forgiveness; we can only repent, for this is the only way to secure forgiveness. No sacrifice or ceremony can bring about forgiveness. Repentance is the only way.

THE HOLY SPIRIT IS POURED OUT UPON THE PENITENT

'Repent … and you shall receive the gift of the Holy Spirit' (Acts 2:38). Impenitence keeps back the full incoming of the Holy Spirit to the heart. To experience the full blessings of God the Holy Spirit there must be a full repentance.

The call to repentance

The call to repentance is universal—necessary for all people and for all sins. If we do not repent we shall perish (Luke 13:5). God 'commands all men everywhere to repent' (Acts 17:30). It is necessary for leaders to repent, for they show the way and can lead communities or countries either upwards in decency and morality or downwards onto the paths of degradation and immorality.

Sinners in general need to repent, for the whole fabric of society is in danger of being fractured and broken. The Bible is no longer regarded as being of any consequence. Faith has fled as people turn to humanism, paganism or simply nothing at all. There is very little respect for authority; older people are treated contemptuously; children are allowed to 'do their own thing', to swear at their teachers and worse; consciences are hardened and goods are taken from employers without any feelings of dishonesty; drink is taken copiously with the attendant problems of accidents and robberies; drugs are a curse, as folk get drawn into the net of crime to gain money to pay for drugs and further ruin their lives; immorality blights the lives of those who plunge recklessly into its wickedness, with its diseases which maim and kill; abuse of children continues unchecked; marriages are dashed and broken on the rocks of self-will and belligerence, while some merely shack up together; others adopt 'alternative' lifestyles, adopting children into weird worlds of unnatural behaviour; crime increases and lives are left scarred and damaged. What a trail of blighted hopes, broken hearts, broken homes, broken lives sin has left us all! Repent of all this wickedness! Repent and turn to God!

There are those who have nothing to do with gross sins and would turn away from all that would appear wicked and unwholesome. They are good, kind, helpful, decent citizens. They see no need to repent, for they do not see that they are culpable or guilty. But morality falls short of heaven; it is only nature refined. Good living is no substitute for salvation. Though the life may be moralized and Christianized, the heart has not been transformed and cleansed. Morality is insufficient. The moral man therefore needs to repent. Don't depend on your goodness any longer. Repent and turn to God!

There are those who are moral and good, and in addition have religion. They think that, because they go to church and enter into all that the church organizes, they are part of those who will inherit eternal life, but they are actually still strangers to the promises of God and are outside the covenant of grace. Religion cannot save you. You need more than religion: you need Christ! Repent of your reliance on your religion and find reality in Christ himself. Repent and turn to God! In true repentance, you will find joy and peace in believing.

Notes

1 *The Westminster Shorter Catechism*, q. 87: 'What is repentance unto life?'

2 **Thomas Watson,** *The Doctrine of Repentance* (1668; 2002, Edinburgh: Banner of Truth), p. 18.

3 **Kenneth S. Wuest,** *Word Studies in the Greek New Testament*, vol. iii (Grand Rapids, MI: Eerdmans, 1983), p. 27.

4 **Louis Berkhof,** *A Summary of Christian Doctrine* (1938; 1968, London: Banner of Truth), p. 122.

5 Quoted in **Ernest S. Williams,** *Systematic Theology*, vol. ii (Springfield, MO: Gospel Publishing House, 1953), p. 235.

6 **Wesley L. Duewel,** *God's Great Salvation* (Greenwood, IN: OMS International, 1991), p. 80.

7 **Sinclair Ferguson,** *The Grace of Repentance* (Wheaton, IL: Crossway, 2000), p. 14.

8 **William Evans,** *The Great Doctrines of the Bible* (1912; 1972, Chicago: Moody Press), p. 141.

9 **Wayne Grudem,** *Bible Doctrine* (1999; 2002, Leicester: IVP), p. 309.

10 *The Westminster Confession of Faith*, XV:ii.

Justification: God's declarative act of pardon

Definitions of justification

- 'Justification may be defined as that legal act of God by which he declares the sinner righteous on the basis of the perfect righteousness of Christ' (Louis Berkhof).[1]
- 'Justification is that judicial or declarative act of God by which he pronounces those who believingly accept the propitiatory offering of Christ as absolved from their sins, released from their penalty, and accepted as righteous before him' (Orton Wiley).[2]
- 'Justification is an act of God's free grace, wherein he pardoneth all our sins, and accepteth us as righteous in his sight, only for the righteousness of Christ imputed to us, and received by faith alone' (*Westminster Shorter Catechism*).[3]
- 'Justification is God's gracious judicial act declaring the repentant sinner free from condemnation and the penalty for his sins, righteous through his faith in Christ as Saviour, acceptable to God and entitled to heaven' (Wesley L. Duewel).[4]
- 'Justification is God's act of remitting the sins of guilty men, and accounting them righteous, freely by his grace, through faith in Christ, on the ground, not of their own works, but of the representative law-keeping and redemptive blood-shedding of the Lord Jesus Christ on their behalf' (J. I. Packer).[5]
- 'By justification we mean that judicial act of God by which, on account of Christ, to whom the sinner is united by faith, he declares that sinner to be no longer exposed to the penalty of the law, but to be restored to his favour' (A. H. Strong).[6]
- 'Justification is a most gracious and righteous act of God, whereby he, imputing the righteousness of Christ to a believing sinner, absolveth him from his sins, and accepteth of him as righteous in Christ, and as an heir

of eternal life, to the praise and glory of his own Mercy and Justice'
(Bishop Downhame).7

1. Understanding the biblical position

From the definitions above, we see that justification consists of two
parts: negatively, absolving sinners of their guilt and pardoning their
sins; and positively, reckoning or imputing to sinners the righteousness
of Christ. Pardoned sinners do not leave the law courts despised and in
disrepute but are clad in the righteousness of the One who took upon
himself their sin and its punishment. Justification is more than pardon:
'to justify' means 'to declare righteous'.

To express this idea of righteousness, Paul used the family of Greek
words with the stem *dik*. The great majority of the uses of *dikaioun* (to
justify, acquit, reckon or make righteous) occur in Romans (fifteen
times) and Galatians (eight times). Outside Pauline writings, the verb is
found in the New Testament only eleven times, and most of these
occurrences are irrelevant to the theological issue.

While James does discuss this subject, the justification and
righteousness theme is virtually peculiar to Paul. The distinctive Pauline
meaning is 'to be right with God'.

A correct understanding of this subject is essential. Luther called the
doctrine of justification by faith *articulus stantis aut cadentis
ecclesiae*—the point of belief which determines whether a church stands
or falls.

Roman Catholic scholars regard the *dik* words as meaning *making*
righteous, not *declaring* righteous. According to them, we are being
made righteous all our lives—justification is progressive. According to
Protestants, however, we are declared righteous in an instantaneous
divine act. It is vital to discover the correct meaning of these words, for it
affects our whole understanding and experience of salvation.

'But how can a man be righteous before God?' asked Job (9:1). 'Sirs,
what must I do to be saved?' asked the Philippian jailor (Acts 16:30).
Both men expressed the great question of how man can get right with
God and be sure of his approval. Certainly all humanity, both Jews and
Gentiles, have a need to know God, for the whole human race is in a

sorry plight because of the Fall of man and the subsequent sinfulness of all.

The need for justification

Man is a sinner (Rom 3:23); he is defiled (Eph. 2:1–3). He is doomed, for 'The soul who sins shall die' (Ezek. 18:4). He is damned, for 'the wages of sin is death' (Rom. 6:23). He is dead in his pleasure (1 Tim. 5:6). God silences every voice and declares all the world to be 'guilty before God' (Rom. 3:19). Man's position before God is clear: he is a sinner under condemnation.

He is, furthermore, totally incapable of saving himself. He cannot save himself by religion: 'by the deeds of the law no flesh will be justified in His sight, for by the law is the knowledge of sin' (Rom. 3:20). The law urges us to do good but the perverted will of man is inclined to do evil. Man, then forced by the law to obey it, does so unwillingly and sees just how deeply sin is rooted within him. He would never notice this if he did not have the law, but now the evil is exposed—the law reveals sin.

Paul says clearly in Galatians, 'For as many as are of the works of the law are under the curse; for it is written, "Cursed is everyone who does not continue in all things which are written in the book of the law, to do them"' (Gal. 3:10). It is taken for granted that man cannot keep the law and that, if he tries, he fails and is condemned by the law. Paul equally plainly states that 'a man is not justified by the works of the law but by faith in Jesus Christ' (Gal. 2:16).

We cannot save ourselves by good works: 'not by works of righteousness which we have done, but according to His mercy He saved us' (Titus 3:5); 'you have been saved through faith … not of works, lest anyone should boast' (Eph. 2:8–9).

Neither our adherence to the law nor our attempt at good works will bring salvation. God has said, 'I will not justify the wicked' (Exod. 23:7). However earnest our religious activities and however ardent our best endeavours, we have the problem of sin with which to contend. Our dedication to religion and morality, however good it may be, will not remove sin, and because of sin's presence we are condemned before a holy God. There is no escape. We need salvation from Someone outside ourselves.

The manner of justification

THE AUTHOR OF JUSTIFICATION

'[T]here is one God who will justify the circumcised by faith and the uncircumcised through faith' (Rom. 3:30); 'It is God who justifies' (Rom. 8:33). All evangelical biblical scholars declare that justification is that judicial act by which God, on account of a sinner's new faith relationship to Jesus Christ, declares that sinner no longer to be exposed to the penalty of a broken law but restored to divine favour.

God forgives the sins of guilty men and women solely on the grounds of Christ's redemptive work; he is the Author and Architect of the plan of justification.

THE AUTHORITY OF JUSTIFICATION

'And such were some of you. But you were washed, but you were sanctified, but you were justified in the name of the Lord Jesus and by the Spirit of our God' (1 Cor. 6:11)—justified in the Name!

In the Name there is authority. Here lies all the authority of heaven. What a Name he has! He is 'Lord over all' (Rom. 10:12), 'Lord of lords' (1 Tim. 6:15), the 'Mighty God' (Isa. 9:6), 'Redeemer' (Isa. 59:20), 'Saviour' (2 Peter 2:20), and a host more. The Name gives authority. If an ambassador speaks 'in the name' of his country, he speaks with the authority of that country. We are justified in the name of Jesus, who comes from heaven and whose name has the authority of the God of heaven. There is no question as to the authenticity of our justification: it is stamped with divine authority, for it is accomplished in his Name.

In the Name there is also dignity. In 1 Corinthians 6:9–10, Paul speaks of the evils of the unrighteous—adulterers, thieves, drunkards, etc.—then he says, 'And such were some of you. But you were ... justified' (v. 11). What a glorious change has taken place! The vilest of people have become saints. The change is life-transforming. They are new creatures in Christ. Old things have passed away. They love purity and prayer, and reject their old evil practices. They can walk the world with dignity and purpose. They need not hide like criminals, for they have been forgiven and have been introduced to and accepted into the family of God. They have been made new in Christ.

In the Name there is also certainty. There is no doubt about the change: it is obvious to all, it brings its own blessed assurance. Doubts are banished and joy wells up in the transformed and justified soul. Justification is certainly something which can be known and wonderfully experienced. Glad testimony springs from joyful certainty.

THE SCOPE OF JUSTIFICATION

'[T]hrough this Man is preached to you the forgiveness of sins; and by Him everyone who believes is justified from all things from which you could not be justified by the law of Moses' (Acts 13:38–39).

THE FORGIVENESS OF SINS

'But there is forgiveness with You, That You may be feared' (Ps. 130:4). The justified person is the forgiven person. The whole account against the one who believes is wiped out. The rebel asks for mercy and it is granted on the grounds of Calvary. The pardon is abundant, full and free (Isa. 55:7; Eph. 4:32; Micah 7: 18–19).

In wonder lost, with trembling joy,
We take the pardon of our God:
Pardon for sins of deepest dye,
A pardon sealed with Jesus' blood.
Who is a pardoning God like Thee?
Or who has grace so rich and free?
(Samuel Davies, 1723–1761).

THE REMOVAL OF CONDEMNATION

'There is therefore now no condemnation to those who are in Christ Jesus' (Rom. 8:1); 'Who shall bring a charge against God's elect? It is God who justifies. Who is he who condemns? It is Christ who died' (Rom. 8:33–34). In justification, the guilt and punishment are removed and the judge acquits the pardoned sinner. God shows here that he is righteous:

he will not punish the one whom he has forgiven for Christ's sake. Men and women were ungodly but have been forgiven, and therefore the law has nothing against them. They walk free from the divine law court—free from condemnation and punishment.

THE IMPUTATION OF RIGHTEOUSNESS

Forgiven sinners are not like discharged prisoners who carry the stigma of imprisonment with them. Justification means more than acquittal: it is the gaining of a righteousness that is not our own—the righteousness of Christ. Faith in Christ's death brings a person into a relationship with a holy God that only the righteous can enjoy. Such a person is righteous in terms of this relationship.

'For He made Him who knew no sin to be sin for us, that we might become the righteousness of God in Him' (2 Cor. 5:21). This verse clearly asserts that in some sense Jesus took sin upon himself, but at the same time he was sinless. He stood in the place of sinners bearing their sin, their guilt and their doom. In the same way, those who are in him have become the righteousness of God. They are counted righteous because of the imputed righteousness of Christ reckoned to them, and they are truly righteous because of the imparted life of Christ within them; 'we ... become the righteousness of God in Him' (2 Cor. 5:21). He becomes 'THE LORD OUR RIGHTEOUSNESS' (Jer. 23:6).

This is a righteousness which does not depend on the demands of the law but faith: 'But now the righteousness of God apart from the law is revealed ... even the righteousness of God, through faith in Jesus Christ, to all and on all who believe' (Rom. 3:21–22; Phil. 3:9).

THE SPRING OF JUSTIFICATION: GRACE

' ... being justified freely by His grace through the redemption that is in Christ Jesus' (Rom. 3:24). Grace is the fountain and source of justification. It is the free unmerited favour of God. There is nothing in us to merit God's favour. We cannot earn salvation and neither do we deserve it. It is God's free gift (Rom. 11:6). We deserve condemnation and punishment, but God in his mercy forgives us.

Mercy is God not giving us what we deserve. Grace is God giving us what we do not deserve. We don't deserve life or heaven but God gives it to us freely. Spurgeon said,

If I could preach justification to be bought by you at a sovereign apiece, who would go out of this place without being justified? If I could preach justification to you by walking a hundred miles, would we not all be pilgrims tomorrow morning, every one of us? If I could preach justification by whippings and torture, there are very few here who would not whip themselves, and that severely too. But when it is given freely, freely, freely, men turn away.[8]

God does not give freely because he is a kind and big-hearted benefactor. The picture of God as a benign celestial grandfather, sympathetic and tolerant, amiable and accommodating, charitable and complacent, is unbiblical and therefore false. God is holy, righteous and just, and he cannot deal leniently with sin. God is 'of purer eyes than to behold evil, and cannot look on wickedness' (Hab. 1:13). He judges sin mercilessly. He has said, 'The soul who sins shall die' (Ezek. 18:20). That is an eternal decree. He cannot retain his perfect justice if he does not fulfil his word. He cannot remain just and simply pardon sin without punishing the sinner.

But he has found a substitute! Just as surely as the justice of God demands punishment, so the love of God provides a substitute. Jesus went to Calvary, identified himself with our sin and took our punishment. Now, because divine justice has been satisfied, divine mercy can be applied. All because Jesus paid the full penalty for sin, God, in his abundant, overflowing grace, gives and gives and gives salvation freely to all who believingly receive it. 'Grace' surely is the most sublime word in the Christian vocabulary.

THE GROUNDS OF JUSTIFICATION: THE BLOOD

'Much more then, having now been justified by His blood, we shall be saved from wrath through Him' (Rom. 5:9). The death of Christ is the foundation of justification: 'without shedding of blood there is no remission' (Heb. 9:22). Christ's death is more than simply the death of a martyr: it is the culmination and focal point of the types and shadows, the pictures and promises of the Old Testament levitical system of offerings, and by it our sins are not merely covered but put away for ever.

In Christ the biblical pictures of substitution focus. They began in the Garden of Eden, when Adam and Eve had to be clothed in the skins of their substitutionary sacrifice (Gen. 3:21). Are we not clothed in the righteousness of our substitutionary Lamb? When Abraham took the knife to kill his son Isaac on the altar—Isaac being a picture of the submissive Son—God stopped him, and instead Abraham offered the ram caught by its horns in a nearby thicket (Gen. 22:12–13)—probably with a thorny bush around its head! At the Exodus, when the Israelites came out of Egypt, each household sacrificed a lamb and placed its blood on the lintel and doorposts of the house. When the angel of death passed over the land and struck all the firstborn, the Israelites were saved, for judgement had already fallen on the substitutionary lamb (Exod. 12). In the whole levitical system, the offerings which were part and parcel of Israelite life spoke of the offering of Christ. When the temple worship was established, there was a continual burnt offering on the altar, signifying the continual efficacy of the blood of Christ. It is always available. No other religion had a continual burnt offering.

God has established a way by which men and women can approach him. It is by means of a substitutionary sacrifice—and that sacrifice is Christ. He died for our sins according to the Scriptures (1 Cor. 15:3). He died for the ungodly (Rom. 5:6), for sinners (Rom. 5:8), and he is the propitiation for us (Rom. 3:24–25). There is no reconciliation, no justification, except through and by Christ and his substitutionary sacrifice.

THE GUARANTEE OF JUSTIFICATION: THE RESURRECTION

'[Jesus] was delivered up because of our offenses, and was raised because of our justification' (Rom. 4:25). The death of Christ is the basis of our justification, but the resurrection of Christ is the proof that God has accepted the sacrifice which he made for us. Speaking of the early Christians, Faulkner says that Christ's death 'cannot be separated from his resurrection, which first awakened them to a knowledge of its decisive worth for salvation, as well as finally confirmed their faith in Jesus as the Son of God.'[9] Without the resurrection, the death of Christ would have meant nothing to them: 'if Christ is not risen, your faith is futile; you are still in your sins!' (1 Cor. 15:17). It was the resurrection which gave Christians their assurance about Christ (Acts 17:31). By the resurrection, Christ has been exalted to God's right hand to make intercession for us (Rom. 8:34). The saving significance and power of his death can be attained and experienced only as it is sealed by the resurrection. Because Christ was raised from the dead, the Christians realized that his death was their substitutionary sacrifice and the resurrection was God's seal of approval on that sacrifice. Because his death was to accomplish our justification, and because it was successful in its objective, God raised him from the dead; the resurrection proves that all that he set out to accomplish through his death he has in fact accomplished. He 'was raised because of our justification' (Rom. 4:25).

THE PRINCIPLE OF JUSTIFICATION: FAITH

'Therefore, having been justified by faith, we have peace with God through our Lord Jesus Christ' (Rom. 5:1; see also 3:26; 4:5). Faith is the instrument and means of justification. By faith we partake of the benefits of the cross. No one can be saved until he or she appropriates the saving work of Christ. Faith is putting out the hand to receive and taking what is given. It is accepting what Christ has done for us.

Faith is not simply a mental assent to spiritual truths. If the enormous effect of Christ's cross-work is believed, it is life-transforming. It demands surrender of the life to the Saviour and an actual realization of reconciliation and justification. To be justified by faith means, then, a commitment, a right relationship with God, a fresh start; 'the gospel … is the power of God to salvation for everyone who believes' (Rom. 1:16). The gospel compels, charges and arrests, for it is the power of God, and it is that to everyone who exercises faith. The hearing of the gospel is an event, it is an encounter with God. If the gospel is believed, the life is transformed.

Faith is not a feeling, not a mystical intuition, not a psychological state of mind, not self-betterment, not a change of opinion, not a meritorious work. It is trusting Christ alone for salvation, and that trust transfers the benefits of Calvary to the life, changing it completely. It is the indispensable prerequisite for receiving God's great salvation.

The consequences of justification

In Romans 5:1–11, Paul speaks of the wonderful blessings that accrue to the one who is justified by God.

WE ARE SAVED FROM WRATH

'Much more then, having now been justified by His blood, we shall be saved from wrath through Him' (Rom. 5:9; 8:1). This is one of the great verses of Scripture.

God's wrath (Greek: *orge*) is his settled indignation against sin. It expresses his abhorrence and hatred of sin and is the eternal repulsion of evil by good. God cannot be holy without reacting against sin and unrighteousness. Richardson defines God's wrath as 'God's righteous and implacable condemnation of sin in every form'.[10] God's terrible wrath against sin will be revealed and God will judge it with the utmost severity.

But we are saved from wrath! A substitute was found, God's wrath was expressed, the judgement has fallen and we are saved—justified by his blood. The wrath of God still rests on the one who does not believe and who will not receive God's substitute, but the one who believes in the Son of God has everlasting life (John 3:16). We are no longer doomed and damned, we no longer face the awful judgement—we are saved! There is no condemnation to face (Rom. 8:1); we shall not come into judgement but have passed from death into life (John 5:24). God's justifying grace has brought us salvation. We are saved from wrath.

WE HAVE PEACE WITH GOD

'Therefore, having been justified by faith, we have peace with God through our Lord Jesus Christ' (Rom. 5:1).

Those who were formerly in rebellion against God have now been reconciled to him by the death of Jesus Christ. The enmity between the sinner and God has been put away by the cross.

The condemned man has no peace. He is separated from God by his sin. There is enmity between him and God, but through the sacrifice of Christ we have peace from the sting of a disturbed conscience and from the dread of an awful judgement. We have peace of heart through the love of God, peace of mind through the truth of God and peace of soul through the presence of God. Our past is blotted out.

It is not only peace because of his death by which we are justified, but also peace because of his life by which we shall be maintained in a state of salvation; Paul writes that this peace comes through Jesus, 'through whom also we have access by faith into this grace in which we stand, and rejoice in hope of the glory of God' (Rom. 5:2). It is peace from past enmity and peace in future security, because of his death and because of his life. We rejoice (there is joy) in hope (there is expectancy) because we have access to God (there is intimacy), and we stand in his grace (there is stability and certainty).

We have a forgiven past and a glorious future, all because of Jesus Christ who 'is our peace', who 'made peace' and who 'preached peace' (Eph. 2:14–17).

WE HAVE JOY IN GOD

'[We] rejoice in hope of the glory of God' (Rom. 5:2). Peace and joy are the twin blessings of the gospel. Someone once said, 'Peace is joy resting; joy is peace dancing.' Three reasons for this joy are mentioned in Romans 5.

The first is rejoicing in the hope of glory (v. 2). This is not the hopeless hope of a marooned sailor on a desert island, but the certain hope of the returning husband to the comfort of a loving and welcoming wife and home. It is a sure hope and it is certain of fulfilment. This hope speaks of the glory of God—that marvellous salvation which God has in store for those who put their trust in him.

The second reason is suffering (v. 3). This was regarded as the token of true Christianity. It helps to cultivate endurance and steadfastness, developing character and stimulating trust.

The third reason for this joy is God himself (v. 11). The psalmist said,

Chapter 3

'God [is] my exceeding joy' (Ps. 43:4) and 'In Your presence is fullness of joy' (Ps. 16:11).

We rejoice 'with joy inexpressible and full of glory' (1 Peter 1:8); 'the joy of the Lord is your strength' (Neh. 8:10); 'I will joy in the God of my salvation' (Hab. 3:18).

Our joy springs from a right relationship with God. We have been justified by faith and can therefore rejoice in God our Saviour. Joy springing from faith is called the 'joy of faith' (Phil. 1:25) and is a distinguishing characteristic of the Christian. 'For we ... who worship God in the Spirit, rejoice in Christ Jesus' (Phil. 3:3).

WE HAVE ACCESS TO GOD

' ... our Lord Jesus Christ, through whom also we have access by faith into this grace in which we stand, and rejoice in hope of the glory of God' (Rom. 5:2). In Christ 'we have boldness and access with confidence through faith in Him' (Eph. 3:12). We have 'access by one Spirit to the Father' (Eph. 2:18); we have access to a mercy seat to which we are invited to come freely. 'Access' indicates that we have the privilege of approaching someone who is highly placed, someone royal or divine.

The Old Testament provides us with an excellent illustration. Jacob and his sons went to Egypt. They had never seen Pharaoh, nor had he seen them. Their brother Joseph, however, who was in a sense the 'firstborn', stood in Pharaoh's presence. He took them into the palace and introduced them to Pharaoh—they had access! Pharaoh received them, gave them the best of the land and continued to favour them because of their relationship to Joseph (Gen. 46–47). Jesus is our heavenly Joseph. He identifies himself with our cause, and he who is our 'elder brother' takes us, sinners, and introduces us to the Father. God receives us and gives us his blessings and favour.

We 'have access by faith into this grace in which we stand'. The Greek *estekarnen* literally means 'we stand fast or firm'. The access into the full grace of God gives stability and strength.

WE HAVE TRIBULATION

'[W]e also glory in tribulations, knowing that tribulation produces

58 Great Gospel Words

perseverance; and perseverance, character; and character, hope' (Rom. 5:3–4). Tribulation or persecution is part of the Christian's lot. It is the reproach of the cross which he bears; 'all who desire to live godly in Christ Jesus will suffer persecution' (2 Tim. 3:12).

Barrett notes that the Christian exults in afflictions, 'because they humble him and prevent him from having confidence in himself, so that he trusts in God only, and gives glory to him'.[11]

When sufferers recognize that they are weak but God is strong, they will readily seek help from above. Since God's help is sufficient, their faith will be strengthened. This results in patience, fortitude, disciplined endurance and perseverance. The enduring of hardships cheerfully and patiently brings experience and tests and strengthens the character. This in turn makes possible a more vigorous hope. Hendriksen observes that 'perseverance produces proven character … [and] proven character brings about hope'.[12] This hope 'does not disappoint'. It does not cause us to be ashamed, it does not prove illusory. It is set on heaven's reality.

WE ARE HEIRS OF GOD

'[H]aving been justified by His grace we … become heirs according to the hope of eternal life' (Titus 3:7). Those who are justified have become legal heirs of God. We have been adopted into the family of God. Once we were children of wrath; now we are heirs of God (Rom. 8:16–17). Once we were doomed to destruction; now we share God's eternal riches. What an enriching and ennobling salvation it is!

The evidence of justification

FRUIT

'You see then that a man is justified by works, and not by faith only' (James 2:24). Good works are the evidence of faith. If there are no works, it is evident that there is no faith; where there is faith, there will of necessity be works. Works are not the basis but the proof of justification. When good works are observed, it is evident to all that justifying grace has been imparted. The tree is known by its fruit.

VICTORY

We reign in life. 'For if by the one man's offense death reigned through the one, much more those who receive abundance of grace and of the gift of righteousness will reign in life through the One, Jesus Christ' (Rom. 5:17). Those who were once reigned over by the tyrant death shall now reign in life. The reasoning of the apostle is bold. The power of sin which dragged him into evil and bondage becomes the proof of the fact that those who trust in the grace of God through Jesus Christ will most certainly be raised to the throne. If you are sure of the fact that death and sin reigned over you, much more—much, much more—will the righteousness you receive in Christ raise you to the throne, and you will reign. 'A new, holy, inexhaustible and victorious vitality will pervade those receivers of righteousness, and make them so many kings. If the collective condemnation could make each of them a subject of death, the conclusion therefore should be that their individual justification will make each of them a king in life.'[13]

In conclusion:

- Judicially, we are justified by God: 'It is God who justifies' (Rom. 8:33).
- Meritoriously, we are justified by Christ: 'My righteous Servant shall justify many' (Isa. 53:11).
- Instrumentally, we are justified by faith: 'Therefore, having been justified by faith … ' (Rom. 5:1).
- Evidentially, we are justified by works: 'What does it profit, my brethren, if someone says he has faith but does not have works?' (James 2:14).

2. Defending the biblical position
'I am appointed for the defense of the gospel' (Phil. 1:17).

Old Testament background
Paul's doctrine of justification can be understood only against the background of the Old Testament.

The righteousness of God in the matter of justification is that it is essentially a legal and forensic act: 'I have prepared my case, I know that I shall be vindicated' (Job 13:18; see also Job 40:8). 'Shall not the Judge of all the earth do right?' (Gen. 18:25). God is pictured as the judge of mankind (Ps. 9:4; 33:5; Jer. 11:20). A righteous person is someone whom the Judge declares to be acquitted in judgement, who is therefore free from guilt and who stands in a right relationship with God (see Exod. 23:7; Deut. 25:1; Job 27:5; Prov. 17:15; Isa. 5:23; 50:8).

Righteousness then flows from the right relationship with a righteous God. Israel had to reflect the righteousness of God. Good living is related to and is the result of the pronouncement of justification. Snaith says that the Hebrew verb translated 'to be righteous' (*tsadaq*) means 'to declare righteous' or 'to justify'.[14]

Justification is not making men and women righteous, but declaring them to be free from guilt. It is a judicial act.

The Roman Catholic understanding of justification
The Roman Catholic Church as we know it today was formed at the Council of Trent which sat for eighteen years in the mid-sixteenth century. In the Tridentine Decrees of 1547, the Roman Church defined its position in opposition to the Reformers. It stated, 'Justification is not the remission of sins alone, but also the sanctification and renewal of the inner man … [We are] not only reckoned, but are truly … righteous, receiving righteousness in us.'[15] The Council of Trent stated, 'If anyone shall say that justifying faith is nothing but confidence in the divine mercy remitting sin on account of Christ, or that this faith is the sole thing by which we are justified; let him be accursed.'[16]

The holding of this position caused the Council, in two other statements, to deny both the instantaneity and the assurance of justification. Justification therefore became a process in which one would grow more and more: a gradual process of the infusion of righteousness in man's nature. Accordingly, justification and sanctification have become confused. Justification has become part of the *process* of salvation.

Protestant doctrines, however, declare with one voice that justification signifies not being *made* righteous (from being wicked), but being *pronounced* righteous. It is an instantaneous event, not a lifelong process. The Roman Catholic position is that, in justifying the sinner, righteousness is imparted, and that justification covers God's whole work of pardoning and sanctifying grace. Doing good deeds therefore has merit and is necessary alongside God's saving work in Christ.

From a biblical viewpoint, sinners need justification from God in a definite act of faith together with the regenerative power of God's Spirit within to make them new creatures in Christ. Thereafter, the sanctifying influences of the indwelling Spirit work in their lives, conforming them to Christ throughout their lives. Sanctification, a lifelong process, follows justification, which is an instantaneous event.

If sinners who have no assurance of justification seek to implement the process of sanctification, believing this to be the justifying grace of God working its process in their lives, they are deceived, having no basis, no foundation and no transformation. They try to become new creatures in Christ and attempt to please God when they have never had a life-transforming encounter in which they have been instantaneously justified and declared righteous. They are attempting to be sanctified without being justified.

Against this background we can understand those who have made enormous sacrifices for Christ when they, in actual fact, have never known his instantaneous justifying grace. They are attempting to work out their own salvation in expressing through their lives the good works which they believe have merit and by which they think that God is infusing righteousness within them. They believe that God is making them righteous as they do good deeds, and that by this they are experiencing God's justifying grace. Their salvation includes the merit of good works. In fact, Bellarmin says, 'The common judgment of all Catholics is, that the good works of the righteous are meritorious … and that they merit … eternal life itself.'[17]

No wonder Luther called the doctrine of justification the mark of the standing or falling church.

Proving justification to be a declaration, not a lifelong process

A CORRECT UNDERSTANDING OF *JUSTIFICARE*

It was the Latin word *justificare*, the translation of the Greek *dikaiousthai* (righteousness), that stood in the way of the right understanding of the gospel. The Pauline word had been taken from the law courts: the accused is acquitted of guilt and declared to be innocent. Unfortunately, around 400 AD Augustine of Hippo, who studied the Bible in Latin, understood *justificare* to mean 'make righteous'. The medieval scholars followed and understood justification as pardon plus inner renewal, as the Roman Catholic Council of Trent in the mid-sixteenth century was also to do. Sanctification was introduced in the realm of justification and confused with it.

Medieval theology thought that the event of this *justificare* should be somehow equated with the sacramental *infusio gratiae* (infusion of grace) which they believed occurred at baptism. 'It was the decisive insight of Luther that he discovered the Hebrew and Pauline meaning of "justificare": which had been completely buried and concealed by the Catholic sacramental tradition of many centuries.'[18]

Justification is not an *infusio gratiae* (infusion of grace) but God's declaration: 'You are right with me.' But the Roman Catholic understanding is that grace is infused at infant baptism and justification is then part of the experience whereby I am made righteous. Because of this, the works which I do are inspired by infused grace which has merit. Good works are therefore part of the justifying process.

THE USE OF THE WORD 'JUSTIFY'

The word 'justify' does not mean 'to make righteous', just as 'to glorify God' does not mean 'to *make* God glorious' but 'to *declare* him glorious'.

'To sanctify the Lord God in our hearts' does not mean 'to *make* him holy' but 'to *declare* him holy'.

God is said to be 'justified' (Luke 7:29), and Christ also (1 Tim. 3:16); they were not made righteous, but declared to be righteous.

Concerning the word 'justify', 'wherever it is used with reference to our acceptance with God, it can only be understood in a judicial or forensic sense,' says Buchanan.[19] Sinners are accepted and justified on the grounds of Christ's righteousness imputed to them, not by their personal righteousness through good works within them.

JUSTIFICATION SET AGAINST CONDEMNATION

In the Bible, the Hebrew and Greek verbs denoting 'justification' are invariably set against those denoting 'condemnation'. 'With reference to the judgments of men, justification is always opposed to condemnation.'[20] For example, in Deuteronomy 25:1 we read, 'If there is a dispute between men, and they come to court, that the judges may judge them, and they justify the righteous and condemn the wicked … ' (see also Prov. 17:15; Isa. 5:23). 'Justification', therefore, no more signifies the infusion of righteousness than 'condemnation' signifies the infusion of wickedness. If condemnation is given instantaneously, then so also is justification.

'Justification' and 'condemnation' denote judicial sentences directly opposed to each other. For example, in Matthew 12:37 we read, 'by your words you will be justified, and by your words you will be condemned' (see also Rom. 8:33–34; 5:16).

If justification is the opposite of condemnation, it can only be, like the latter, a judicial and forensic pronouncement instantly given. It is not a term which indicates gradual betterment and character refinement.

ASSOCIATED TERMS IMPLY THE JUDICIAL SCENE

Buchanan's argument is good:

All the … terms, with which justification is associated … designate … circumstances which are implied in a process of judgment.

In connection with it we read:

of a Judgment: 'Enter not into judgment with thy servant; for in thy sight shall no man living be justified' (Ps. 143:2);

of a Judge: 'Shall not the Judge of all the earth do right?' (Gen. 18:25); 'We are sure that the judgment of God is according to truth' (Rom. 2:2);

of a Tribunal: 'We shall all stand before the judgment seat of Christ' (Rom. 14:10);

of an Accuser: 'Who shall lay any thing to the charge of God's elect? It is God that justifieth' (Rom. 8:33);

of an Indictment: 'Forgiving you all trespasses; blotting out the handwriting of ordinances that was against us, which was contrary to us' (Col. 2:14–14) …

and of a sentence of Absolution: 'Blessed is he whose transgression is forgiven, whose sin is covered. Blessed is the man unto whom the LORD imputeth not iniquity' (Ps. 32:1–2).

All these expressions imply a judicial act, and they are correlative to (and associated with) the term Justification.[21]

This is not a lifelong process; it is an instantaneous judgement. It is not an absorption of divine qualities over a lifetime; it is a divine forensic act whereby the sinner is acquitted in a moment. The scene is that of the judgement hall.

EQUIVALENT EXPRESSIONS DO NOT IMPLY INFUSION OF RIGHTEOUSNESS

Expressions equivalent in meaning to 'justification' denote forgiveness and acceptance of the sinner and show justification to be a change in the sinner's judicial relation to God, not a change in his or her moral character. '[Abraham] believed in the LORD, and He accounted it to him for righteousness' (Gen. 15:6). That took place when God promised him children. 'Blessed is the man to whom the LORD does not impute iniquity'

(Ps. 32:2); 'God was in Christ reconciling the world to Himself, not imputing their trespasses to them' (2 Cor. 5:19); 'For He made Him who knew no sin to be sin for us, that we might become the righteousness of God in Him' (2 Cor. 5:21). These verses show that justification can mean nothing else than the acceptance of the sinner as righteous in the sight of God.

We can now say with conviction that the word 'justify' is a judicial term meaning to acquit, to declare righteous, to pronounce the sentence of acceptance. It is a change in a person's relation or standing before God, who declares that person to be free from the consequences of his or her sins and restored to his favour. On God's part it is an act of declaration; on man's part it is an act of reception—by faith. It is first a subtraction: the cancellation of sins; and then, an addition: the imputation of righteousness.

It is instantaneous, in that it is a definite pronouncement as a result of an act of faith.

It is personal, in that it is experienced only by those who seek to find this grace themselves.

It is comprehensive, in that it is the forgiveness of all the sins of the past.

Is justification fictitious?

This conclusion, however, raises a query. Does justification by faith, whereby the righteousness of Christ is reckoned to sinners, mean that sinners are treated as if they were righteous when in fact they are not?

While justification is a forensic term whereby the guilt and condemnation attached to sin are removed by the Judge, it is important to note that the one who is so justified is also forgiven. This Protestant doctrine has been accused of antinomianism, a declarative act not changing the person, who continues in his or her old sinful ways. Justification, however, is only one aspect of salvation. God not only forgives in an instant of submission and confession, but he also imparts his life to believers, and this transforms them.

If justification were solely a legal pronouncement without the accompanying work of the Spirit, the 'standing' and 'state' of the believer could be widely separated, and the dangerous perversions of antinomianism could lead a soul to trust merely in the imputed righteousness of Christ without inner transformation. It would then be a fictitious righteousness, sinners claiming to be something that they are not. They would still be in their sins while falsely claiming Christ's righteousness.

The new life received in the act of justifying faith and regenerating grace alleviates this danger and guides the soul into God's sanctifying grace. At justification, inward sanctification begins.

God forgives in a sovereign act and justifies in a forensic act, all because of the one sacrifice of Jesus Christ. Believing sinners have their sins forgiven and are actually cleansed while the guilt and condemnation are removed by the declaration of the Judge in God's law court; 'let it be known to you, brethren, that through this Man is preached to you the forgiveness of sins; and by Him everyone who believes is justified from all things from which you could not be justified by the law of Moses' (Acts 13:38–39).

Not only is the condemnation removed, but also the reason for the condemnation, man's sin, is forgiven. Justification consists therefore in the remission of sin and the removal of guilt and condemnation. It is therefore not legal fiction.

Believing justification to be a fictitious righteousness is erroneous. The forensic righteousness of justification is a real righteousness. A person's relationship to God is not fiction. God does not treat sinners as though they were righteous; the sinners are, in fact, righteous. Through Christ, they have entered a new relationship with God and are righteous in terms of this relationship.

Justification thus means forgiveness and freedom from condemnation and punishment. Sinners are absolved and acquitted. They have no debt to pay, no penalty to fear, no condemnation to face. They are before God as if they had never sinned. They are saved. All has been taken care of by the substitutionary death of Christ upon the cross. He, God's sinless Son, fulfilled the demands of God's holiness, law and justice in dying in our place; 'who Himself bore our sins in His own body on the tree, that we, having died to sins, might live for righteousness—by whose stripes you were healed' (1 Peter 2:24).

Christ's righteousness is now reckoned to sinners, is imputed to them; they become righteous in Christ and enter into a new relationship with the righteous and holy God who is now their present Saviour, saving them not only by his death but also by his indwelling righteous life.

JUSTIFICATION INVOLVES IMPUTING

Christ's righteousness is imputed to believers. What does this entail?

Imputation is an act of God as sovereign Judge, at once judicial and sovereign, whereby: (1) he makes the guilt and legal responsibilities of our sins really Christ's and punishes him for them; (2) he makes the righteousness of Christ ours and then treats us as persons legally invested with those rights.

The righteousness of Christ is imputed to those who are actually forgiven. It is reckoned to them. Our sins were taken by Christ—were put to his account—and removed on the cross. We are forgiven and the condemnation is removed. His righteousness is taken by God who puts it to our account; and we stand before God, declared righteous in Christ.

Justifying faith is the initial act of the Christian life and it is accompanied by an inward spiritual change known as regeneration. Faith unites the believer to the living Christ and this entails a change of heart, when our sins are forgiven. Righteousness is imputed in justification and imparted in regeneration. The Christ who died for us becomes the Christ who lives in us.

Christ perfectly kept the law (Rom. 10:4) and hence is the only one against whom there has been no cause for condemnation. When my sins are forgiven, God reckons to me Christ's perfect life which merits no condemnation. There is therefore no condemnation upon me, firstly, because my sins have been forgiven, and secondly, because the life I now live is his life upon which there never was condemnation.

His righteousness is imputed to me, but it is also a real righteousness imparted to me by his indwelling Spirit. On the one hand, it is legal, the righteousness of a justifying act, and on the other, it is regenerative, the righteousness of an imparted life.

God sovereignly forgives, forensically justifies and paternally regenerates. I am then a new creature in Christ Jesus.

JUSTIFICATION IS NOT BY WORKS

PAUL AND JAMES (ROM 3:21–26; JAMES 2:14–26)

It has often been said that the writings of Paul and James on the issue of justification are contradictory, Paul saying that justification is by faith, and James, that it is by works; but this is to misunderstand the teaching of James.

Faith is opposed to works when by 'works' we mean good deeds upon which a person depends for salvation. A living, true faith will reveal itself in good works, just as a living apple tree will produce apples. The evidence that faith is present is that works are produced. Works are the result of faith and are the observed consummation of faith. James commends the works that show that faith is present. Paul rejects works as the means of acceptance by God. Works in themselves do not justify, but they are evident when faith is present.

The difference between the presentations of Paul and James is due to the nature of those whom they opposed. Paul contended with legalists who wanted to base their justification, at least in part, on the works of the law; therefore he stressed that justification is by faith. James was dealing with those who claimed to have faith but who denied the necessity of good works; therefore he stressed that without works the faith of which they boasted was dead.

James does not deny salvation to him who has faith, but only to him who falsely professes to have it. Works are an outward manifestation of an inward grace: they prove that grace is present. Paul is describing the instrument of justification: faith; James is describing the nature of faith: it results in works. Paul instructs the seeker as to the method of justification: faith; and James exposes the false believer who claims salvation but whose lack of works proves that he or she does not possess it. Paul teaches the same truth often: 'faith [works] through love' (Gal. 5:6); 'love is the fulfillment of the law' (Rom. 13:10).

Abraham is said to have been 'justified by works when he offered Isaac' (James 2:21). It is quite evident that James is not speaking of the justification of the sinner, for Abraham the sinner was justified around forty years before this incident. James is not speaking of his pardon and acceptance by God, but stating that his act of offering Isaac was a declaration, a manifestation, a satisfactory proof, that he had living faith.

In Romans 4, Paul uses the great illustration of Abraham as an example of one who is justified by faith. James speaks of his offering of Isaac as an affirmation of his faith, a revelation of the truth, an evidence of the reality of his faith. He was proved to be what he had previously been declared to be. We are justified by faith alone, but the faith that justifies is never alone.

PROOF THAT WORKS CANNOT BE THE GROUNDS OF JUSTIFICATION

Paul asserts that we are 'not justified by the works of the law but by faith' (Gal. 2:16) and we are not justified by our own righteousness which comes by obedience to the law (Phil. 3:9). He uses various arguments to establish this position.

- Our works are not perfect, therefore they lead to condemnation (Gal. 3:10,21; 5:3).
- If we are justified by works, Christ died in vain (Gal. 2:21; 5:4).
- If justification were of works, it would not be of grace (Rom. 11:6; Eph. 2:8–9).
- If it were based on works, it would afford cause for boasting (Rom. 3:27; 4:2).
- The Old Testament shows that all people are sinners (Rom. 3:9–10); consequently, none can be justified by works (Ps. 143:2; Rom. 3:20). Habakkuk 2:4 proves that the just shall live by faith, as does the example of Abraham (Gal. 3:6).

Surely if I must rely partly on my own works for salvation, three questions arise: Could I ever do enough? When would I have done enough? How would I know when I had done enough?

JUSTIFICATION IS BY FAITH

The grace of justification is received by faith (Rom. 1:17). There is no merit in this faith any more than a drowning man is to be praised for grasping the rope that is thrown to him or a beggar is to be commended for holding out his hand for a gift. We are to do nothing for God's gift, we are only to take it. This taking and receiving is faith and faith links us to Christ and all his riches. Faith is the instrumental cause of justification.

Faith is not a meritorious work. It is not the cause or basis of justification. If we wish to cross the ocean by ship, we board the ship, placing trust in the captain to take us across. It is not our faith in the captain that takes us across the ocean, but the captain's skill. There is nothing to commend in our trust in the skilled captain, but it is nevertheless necessary for us first of all to commit ourselves to the ship and the captain. In the same sense, as we commit ourselves to Christ by faith, he justifies us by his grace. There is nothing to commend in the act of our trusting our great Captain; however, it is necessary to do so to make the journey from earth to heaven. It requires a trust and a committal.

We are never said to be justified 'on account of faith', only 'through faith' (*dia pisteos*, Rom. 3:25) and 'by faith' (*ek pisteos*, Rom. 3:26). If we were justified 'on account of faith' (*dia pistin*), because it would be a meritorious work of obedience, we would be justified by works; yet Paul never uses that phrase.

Faith is not a work to be commended; faith is the receptive attitude and energetic principle by which salvation is imparted to the soul. Faith is not the grounds of justification, but the means by which it comes.

Justifying faith centres on Christ and his sacrifice, and God and his promises. In its very essence, therefore, it involves trust, and, denying its own worth, affirms the merit of that on which it trusts. Faith in itself, therefore, has no merit. It is merely the instrument by which we are justified by his grace.

While human works are bankrupt of value in attaining salvation, faith is personal trust in and total commitment to Jesus Christ and all that he did on Calvary to procure salvation. Faith is not just a mental comprehension and assent to spiritual truths, but a moral appropriation, a reception of the truths that results in a total surrender of the whole being to Christ. It is trusting Christ alone for salvation, committing ourselves completely to him.

Hunter describes several characteristics of faith:[22]

- Faith is directed not to a proposition, but to a person (God—1 Thes. 1:8; Christ—Col. 2:5).

- As a principle of salvation, faith is opposed to works (Gal. 2:16; 3:3; Rom. 4:5; etc.).
- It is at once an act (Rom. 10:9) and an attitude of life (Gal. 2:20). It is not merely to say once, 'I believe in Christ'; rather it is to go on believing and living that faith.
- Faith is, in Luther's figure, the Christian's 'wedding ring', for it so unites a man to Christ that he enters mystically and morally into all that Christ has done for him (Rom. 6:3–14), so that he dwells in Christ and Christ in him (Gal. 2:20; 2 Cor. 13:5; Eph. 3:17).
- Faith issues in good works. It is the outflowing of God's life and love (Gal. 5:6).

Notes

1 **Louis Berkhof,** *Manual of Christian Doctrine* (Grand Rapids, MI: Eerdmans, 1933), p. 256.

2 **Orton Wiley,** *Introduction to Christian Theology* (Kansas City, MO: Beacon Hill, 1963), p. 276.

3 *The Westminster Shorter Catechism*, q. 33: 'What is justification?'

4 **Wesley L. Duewel,** *God's Great Salvation* (Greenwood, IN: OMS International, 1991), p. 118.

5 **J. I. Packer** in **J. D. Douglas** (ed.), *The New Bible Dictionary* (London: IVP, 1962), p. 649.

6 **A. H. Strong,** *Systematic Theology* (London: Pickering & Inglis, 1907), p. 849.

7 **Bishop Downhame** in **James Buchanan,** *The Doctrine of Justification* (1867; 1961, Edinburgh: Banner of Truth), p. 233.

8 Quoted in **J. Clyde Turner,** *Soul-winning Doctrines* (Nashville, TN: Southern Baptist, 1943), p. 74.

9 **J. A. Faulkner** in **J. Orr** (ed.), *International Standard Bible Encyclopedia*, vol. iii (1939; 1976, Grand Rapids, MI: Eerdmans), p. 1783.

10 **A. Richardson,** *An Introduction to the Theology of the New Testament* (London: SCM, 1938), p. 224.

11 **C. K. Barrett,** *The Epistle to the Romans* (Black's NT Commentary; London: Adam & Charles Black, 1962), p. 103.

12 **W. Hendriksen,** *Romans 1–8* (Edinburgh: Banner of Truth, 1980), pp. 170,177.

13 **F. L. Godet,** *Commentary on Romans* (1914; 1983, Grand Rapids, MI: Kregel), p. 223.

14 **N. Snaith,** *Distinctive Ideas of the Old Testament* (New York: Schocken Books, 1968), p. 73.

15 Quoted in **J. Banks,** *A Manual of Christian Doctrine* (5th edn.; London: Charles Kelly, 1895), p. 170.

16 Quoted in **Wiley,** *Introduction to Christian Theology*, p. 279.

17 Quoted in **Banks,** p. 177.

18 E. Brunner, *Dogmatics*, vol. iii (London: Lutterworth, 1962), p. 209.

19 Buchanan, *Doctrine of Justification*, p. 227.

20 Ibid. p. 229.

21 Ibid. p. 230.

22 A. M. Hunter, *Interpreting Paul's Gospel* (London: SCM, n.d.), p. 33.

Regeneration: the new birth

Definitions of regeneration

- 'Regeneration is that act of God by which the principle of the new life is implanted in man, and the governing disposition of the soul is made holy' (Louis Berkhof).[1]
- 'He "begets us" to himself (James 1:18); "we are born of God", by an inward communication of his nature to us' (Robert Candlish).[2]
- 'Regeneration or Conversion is that great change which God the Holy Spirit works in the heart of a penitent sinner at the same time that he forgives his sins. It is of the nature of a new birth; it is the beginning of a new spiritual life, the soul starting life afresh with everything new' (*The Salvation Army Handbook of Doctrine*).[3]
- '"Regeneration" or "new birth" describes the inner renewal by the Spirit of God which takes place when a person becomes a Christian. It relates the Christian to God and to fellow believers' (H. Burkhardt).[4]
- 'Regeneration or the new birth is the instrument that brings us into the family of God, into the kingdom of the Son of God. It is the creation by the Holy Spirit of a new life in man called the "new creation", or the "new man". Like the first birth it is an event not a process' (Alban Douglas).[5]
- 'Regeneration is the work of the Holy Spirit in the heart of the sinner as he repents and turns to Christ for salvation. By regeneration his soul which had been dead in transgression and sins is made alive by the Holy Spirit. In the same moment that he is forgiven and justified he is resurrected out of spiritual death. He is given new spiritual life and becomes a new creature in Christ Jesus' (Wesley L. Duewel).[6]
- 'By regeneration we are admitted to the kingdom of God. There is no other way of becoming a Christian but by being born from above. In regeneration we are made partakers of the divine nature. We have put on the new man, which after God is created in holiness and righteousness. Christ now lives in the believer. Regeneration is a crisis with a view to a process' (William Evans).[7]

- 'Regeneration is the act by which new life is given. In the evangelical doctrine of salvation it is applied to the instantaneous change from spiritual death to spiritual life' (E. F. Kevan).[8]
- 'Regeneration is God's act in the soul. It is the introduction of a new life. It is the inward expression of which conversion should be the outward expression. It involves a radical change of the profoundest character. It is a condition of becoming "alive from the dead". There comes through the creative act of the Holy Spirit a participation in the life of Christ, membership of the body of which he is the Head, union with the Vine' (Herbert Lockyer).[9]
- 'A spiritual resurrection has taken place. This regeneration causes a complete revolution in man. The change is so radical that it is possible to speak of a "new creature", of a "new man, that after God hath been created in righteousness and holiness and truth". Regeneration, being a new birth, is the starting point of spiritual growth' (John L. Nuelson).[10]
- 'Regeneration is a creation not a transformation; the bringing in of a new thing, not the change of an old; the old nature remains unchanged, but regeneration is the incoming of another nature' (Robert Lee).[11]
- 'Regeneration, or the new birth, is an inner re-creating of fallen human nature by the gracious sovereign action of the Holy Spirit. It is a radical and complete transformation wrought in the soul by God the Holy Spirit by virtue of which we become new men, no longer conformed to this world, but in knowledge and holiness of the truth created after the image of God. Regeneration is the "birth" by which this work of new creation is begun' (J. I. Packer).[12]
- 'Regeneration is the Divine act which imparts to the penitent believer the new and higher life in personal union with Christ' (Myer Pearlman).[13]
- 'Regeneration is that act of God by which the governing disposition of the soul is made holy, and by which, through the truth as a means, the first holy exercise of this disposition is secured. Regeneration, or the new birth, is the divine side of that change of heart which, viewed from the human side, we call conversion' (A. H. Strong).[14]
- 'Regeneration is the inward quickening of the repentant and believing

sinner from spiritual death to spiritual life which occurs in Christian conversion. As such it is simultaneous with the other aspects of this religious experience, viz., justification, adoption and initial sanctification' (Harold B. Kuhn).[15]
- 'Justification is with a view to reigning in life, and is spoken of as "justification of life" (Rom. 5:18). From the divine side, the change of heart is called regeneration, the new birth; from the human side, it is called conversion. In regeneration, the soul is passive; in conversion, it is active. Regeneration may be defined as the communication of divine life to the soul; as the impartation of a new nature or heart, and the production of a new creation' (Henry C. Thiessen).[16]
- 'The new birth is a passing out of death into life, the impartation of life to men dead through trespasses and sins. It is wrought by the Word of God and the Spirit of God. It is the impartation of a new nature, even God's own nature, to the one who is begotten again' (R. A. Torrey).[17]
- 'Regeneration is the communication of life by the Spirit to a soul dead in trespasses and sins' (Orton Wiley).[18]
- 'Regeneration is the incoming of divine life making him who is regenerated "partaker of the divine nature"' (Ernest S. Williams).[19]

What regeneration is not

IT IS NOT BAPTISM
Baptism is an outward sign of an inward experience. Passages such as John 3:5 ('unless one is born of water and the Spirit …') and Titus 3:5 ('the washing of regeneration') refer neither to physical water nor to water baptism. There are several options as to what Christ meant when he used these words. 'Born of water' could mean:
- *Natural birth*. A baby is carried in water in its mother's womb, so we have the natural birth preceding the spiritual birth. We are born of water naturally, and of the Spirit spiritually.
- *Repentance*. This conversation between Jesus and Nicodemus took place at the beginning of Jesus' ministry, so the life and message of John the Baptist were still in the minds of the people. John's was a

baptism of repentance so, in essence, Jesus was saying, 'You must be born of water, signifying repentance, and the Spirit.'

- *The cleansing power of the Word of God.* Note Ephesians 5:26: 'the washing of water by the word'; and John 15:3: 'You are already clean because of the word ... '
- *The whole message of the gospel and its cleansing power.* Water is the emblem of spiritual washing; it is not the washing itself. It is the impact of the purity of the message of the gospel upon those who receive it.

Even if it were supposed that water baptism is the means by which we enter heaven, the text still says that we must be born of water and the Spirit. Even physical water is not sufficient.

Although Paul was the spiritual father of the Corinthian Christians (1 Cor. 4:15), he states clearly that he baptized none of them except Crispus and Gaius (1 Cor. 1:14). They did not receive spiritual birth through baptism. In Acts 10, Cornelius was saved before he was baptized. The thief on the cross was saved without the rite of baptism.

Sadly, millions of people have depended, and are today depending, on their baptism to get them into heaven, for they think that being sprinkled or immersed by the representative of the church affords them salvation status. Sadly, they will die unsaved in spite of a public ritual.

IT IS NOT CHURCH MEMBERSHIP

Many think that they are safe because they have been confirmed, catechized, instructed and accepted as church members. Their names are on the church roll and that is sufficient proof of their piety and religious inclinations, but having their names on a church roll does not mean that their names are on heaven's roll. Such people understand and accept to a large degree what the Bible teaches. Theirs is a cerebral faith, for they believe with their minds but have not trusted with their hearts. It is a mental comprehension but not yet a moral appropriation. A mental belief in Christ is necessary, but it is only the first step to saving faith, which also requires repentance towards God and faith in Jesus as personal Saviour. Such people believe that, because they have joined the church, they are Christians; sadly they are mistaken.

Church membership, although very good and necessary to those who know Christ, is definitely not the foundation of salvation. It is an outward commitment to a religious body and in itself does not afford an inward spiritual renewal. How sad that so many identify with the outward visible church but do not realize that this does not unite them with the true invisible church, which is Christ's body!

IT IS NOT MERE HUMAN ACHIEVEMENT

Regeneration is not the act of the human will. We are 'born, not ... of the will of the flesh' (John 1:13). The new birth does not come by self-effort. The intellect might well be enlightened by the truth, resulting in a determined imitation of Christ and his teaching, but this will not bring about the new birth. Truth alone is not sufficient. The new birth is effected by the Holy Spirit working in us, not by our strenuous attempts to achieve spirituality. The new birth can never be achieved by human endeavour; it cannot be developed or earned. If we do not have spiritual life, how can we develop what we do not possess? Spiritual life cannot evolve; it is imparted by the Spirit.

IT IS NOT REFORMATION

The consciences of some are finally awakened. They want to leave their drinking, swearing, drugs, immorality and wild parties, and so they turn to better ways. Their outward conduct is changed.

As a young lad under conviction of sin, I tried to break the habit of swearing and, using the knuckle of my right hand, I struck my left forearm whenever I used a bad word—each word had a corresponding number of painful strikes. At times my arm was black and blue! I succeeded, but the better I became outwardly, the less peace I had inwardly. Reformation was not the answer, for it is not the new birth.

What is needed is more than reformation. It is not the turning over of a new leaf but the bringing in of a new life. It is not the improvement of the old nature but the impartation of a new nature. Reformation deals with exterior things but regeneration with interior realities. Reformation alters a person's manner but regeneration alters the whole person. Reformation changes outward conduct but regeneration changes the whole inner being. Reformation is a natural act or process but regeneration is a supernatural work of God in the soul. Reformation may be progressive but regeneration is instantaneous.

'For by grace you have been saved through faith, and that not of yourselves; it is the gift of God, not of works, lest anyone should boast' (Eph. 2:8–9); 'a man is not justified by the works of the law' (Gal. 2:16); 'not by works of righteousness which we have done, but according to His mercy He saved us' (Titus 3:5).

IT IS NOT HEREDITARY

The new birth is 'not of blood' (John 1:13). Regeneration cannot be inherited. No one has an inborn spark of life which need only be developed. My new birth does not depend on my having saintly parents, a relative who is a minister or some other spiritual connection. I cannot inherit divine life from godly associates. It is a personal necessity and a personal responsibility.

IT IS NOT REINCARNATION

A friend of mine was once standing at an open-air meeting while someone was preaching on the new birth. A man next to him listened and in disbelief turned to my friend, saying incredulously, 'Does that young fellow really think that he will return after his death and be born again into this world?' That was a total misunderstanding! No—the new birth is not reincarnation!

In his conversation with Nicodemus, Jesus was certainly speaking of someone in this life when he said, 'You must be born again' (John 3:7). We cannot obey that command after we have died, for the Bible says, 'it is appointed for men to die once, but after this the judgment' (Heb. 9:27). After death comes judgement, not a reincarnated being. The new birth refers to that which takes place in the heart of man in this life, not before birth or after death. The seed must first fall into the field before the harvest can be gathered. The seed is the Word and the field is the hearts of men and women. They are in this life and are thus able to receive the message of life in Christ Jesus and to respond to it.

Chapter 4

IT IS NOT RESTRICTED TO THE DAYS OF JESUS

It has been said that, because Jesus spoke strongly of regeneration and Paul's emphasis was rather on justification, reconciliation and redemption, the matter of the new birth was confined to the days of the Lord Jesus.

This is completely erroneous, as the writers of the New Testament also speak clearly of this doctrine. Peter says, 'God ... has begotten us again to a living hope through the resurrection of Jesus Christ from the dead' (1 Peter 1:3). James speaks of it (James 1:18) and, in his epistles, John speaks several times of the characteristics of those who are 'born of God'. There is therefore no doubt whatsoever that the experience of the new birth is meant for us today.

IT IS NOT CHRISTIAN SERVICE

Some think that, because they are Christian workers, missionaries, ministers or involved in church work even though in secular employment, they are therefore Christians. Jesus, however, said, 'Many will say to Me in that day, "Lord, Lord, have we not prophesied in Your name ... and done many wonders in Your name?" And then I will declare to them, "I never knew you; depart from Me, you who practice lawlessness!"' (Matt. 7:22–23).

It is possible to build our houses on sand (Matt. 7:26–27) and have what we thought of as a stable Christian life and character washed away in the storm of God's judgement. It is possible to have all the outward appearances of being a true Christian and yet be untransformed in our inner natures. Outward goodness is no substitute for inner grace.

The marks of the new birth

RIGHTEOUSNESS

'If you know that He is righteous, you know that everyone who practices righteousness is born of Him' (1 John 2:29). William Barclay says, 'The only way in which he [a man] can prove that he really has had a new birth is by the righteousness of his life. The profession of a man's lips will always be proved or disproved by the practice of his life.'[20]

It does not mean that all right-doing moralists are Christians, but it does mean that because God is righteous, those who are born of him and have his Spirit will practise righteousness in deed and truth. In 1 John 2:29, the implication is that, because we are born of a righteous Father, we practise righteousness. The sentence reveals the lifestyle of those who are born of God. They are children of the righteous Father; as children they will reproduce his character and the family likeness will be recognized. Kistemaker says, 'It explains the reason for the right conduct. Their conduct is right because believers are the children of God.'[21] John Stott says, 'Unrighteous conduct is unthinkable in the Christian.'[22]

PURITY

'Whoever has been born of God does not sin' (1 John 3:9). The Christian and sin are incompatible: 'He who sins is of the devil' (3:8). Bruce says, 'The new birth involves a radical change in human nature; for those who have not experienced it, sin is natural, whereas for those who have experienced it, sin is unnatural—so unnatural, indeed, that its practice constitutes a powerful refutation of any claim to possess the divine life.'[23]

There are three similar statements in 1 John 3: the Christian who abides in Christ 'does not sin' (v. 6); 'He who sins is of the devil' (v. 8); and '[the Christian] cannot sin' (v. 9). In the original Greek, these statements are written in the present tense, indicating not an isolated act but a settled habit of life. This means that, because a person is born of God, he or she is not able to sin continuously. One who is born of God will not persist in sin as a prevailing habit. The words do not mean that it is impossible to commit an act of sin, but rather that those who are born of God find it utterly impossible to persist in sin.

LOVE

'[E]veryone who loves is born of God' (1 John 4:7). The God who is love (4:8) loved us (4:10) and expressed that love by sending his Son to die for us. Stott reminds us that 'while the origin of love is in the being of God the manifestation of love is in the coming of Christ'.[24] Christ so loved that he gave himself for those who actually hated and killed him. He loved them even as they were crucifying him. He loved the unlovely, the sinners, the ones who were cruel, vindictive, filthy, vile. He gave himself to save them from their sin and to bring them to God and to righteousness.

Love, then, is the characteristic of those who are born of God and have his life and nature. It is the expression of his love flowing through them. It is the love of God, not human love, which could never rise to those heights, that is expressed in and through those who are born of God.

In the original Greek there are several words used to express love, but the word used in 1 John 4 is one that speaks of the love of God, that is, *agape* love. It is not human friendship or the love of a man for a woman, but the wonderful, all-embracing love of God indwelling man and expressing itself through man. That is the evidence of being born from above.

SAVING FAITH

'Whoever believes that Jesus is the Christ is born of God' (1 John 5:1). 'Christ' comes from the Greek word used to translate the Hebrew 'Messiah', which means 'anointed'. In the Old Testament, three people were anointed: the prophet, priest and king. Jesus comes as all three. He is the supremely anointed One. As such he institutes salvation for the people. He is the anointed Saviour.

To 'believe' means much more than assenting to the proposition that Jesus is the Saviour or even having a mental acceptance of Jesus as Saviour. It is more than mental comprehension, more than a cerebral faith. It is a relying on, a clinging to, a trusting in, Jesus as that Saviour. It is a moral appropriation. It is an acceptance of Jesus as my own personal Saviour. It means personal faith in him and personal union with him. That is the condition of one who is born of God.

OVERCOMING GRACE

'For whatever is born of God overcomes the world' (1 John 5:4). By using the word 'whatever' (or 'whatsoever') and not 'whoever', John is emphasizing not the victorious person but the victorious power dwelling in that person. It is not man but the life of God in man which conquers. Jesus says, 'I have overcome the world' (John 16:33). His victory becomes ours. We conquer by his power, for his overcoming life is within us. 'He who is in you is greater than he who is in the world' (1 John 4:4).

'The new birth is a supernatural event which takes us out of the sphere of the world, where Satan rules, into the family of God,' says Stott.[25] We have been delivered from the dominion of darkness. The spell of the old life has been broken. The world with its glitter and glow, its attractions and allurements, its fascination and fleshpots, has lost its appeal. The web of sin is broken, the chains are loosed, the captive is free. We 'overcome the world'. It is essentially practical and the result is that the dishonest become honest, drunkards become sober, the corrupt become pure and the immoral are transformed into the humble, holy, repentant and God-fearing servants of God; 'in all these things we are more than conquerors through Him who loved us' (Rom. 8:37).

The motives for the new birth

THE COMMAND OF CHRIST

Jesus said, 'You must be born again' (John 3:7). Hendriksen writes, 'When Jesus says, "You must be born again", he does not mean, "By all means see to it that you are born again." On the contrary, he means, "Something has to happen to you: the Holy Spirit must plant in your hearts the life from above."'[26] The kingdom of heaven is spiritual and we are fleshly, so it is logical that we must be born of the Spirit in order to be spiritual citizens of a spiritual kingdom. It is impossible for us to enter a spiritual heaven without becoming spiritual people, and to be that, we need to be born of the Spirit.

Jesus said, 'That which is born of the flesh is flesh, and that which is born of the Spirit is spirit' (John 3:6). Flesh and spirit belong to different realms. One cannot produce the other. Human nature can produce human nature, but only the Holy Spirit can generate a spiritual nature. It is obvious, therefore, that to be spiritual we must be born of the Spirit.

Jesus said that if we are not born again, we cannot see the kingdom of God (John 3:3). There is no exception to this rule. There is no substitute for the new birth. If we are not born again, we are lost. No age, sex, position, circumstance or condition exempts anyone from this necessity. The universal sinful condition of man demands a change; it demands the new birth for salvation. The natural man is intellectually blind to the truth of his condition. He is corrupt in his affections (Gal. 5:19–21) and perverse in his will (Rom. 8:7). This is the condition of every unregenerate person, no matter how cultured, refined or outwardly moral he or she may be. The holiness of God demands a change in us, for we are sinful and sin cannot stand before the presence of a holy God. Holiness is not to be attained by natural development or self-effort, but by being born of God's Holy Spirit. That is the only way. It is therefore imperative that we are born again.

Nicodemus knew only salvation by good works according to the law, but Jesus confronted the astonished religious teacher with a new concept: religion was not external but internal. It was about receiving spiritual life, not obeying religious laws. It was individual ('you'), it was imperative ('must') and it was internal ('be born again').

If for no other reason than the command of Jesus, we must be born again. Religion is not enough; good works are not enough; doing our best is not enough. I must be born again. Jesus said so. Those who would argue against it argue not with the preacher or with this writer, but with the Lord Jesus Christ, the One who speaks with all the solemnity of eternity and the authority of deity. He is God incarnate and he tells us most emphatically that we must be born again. This is not a mental plaything. It is not optional, but obligatory. This is a command which must be obeyed.

THE CROSS OF CHRIST

'For Christ also suffered once for sins, the just for the unjust, that He might bring us to God, being put to death in the flesh but made alive by the Spirit' (1 Peter 3:18). This was the express purpose of his coming. He was born to die so that others might come to God and live by the life of the resurrected Christ. This life he offers freely to us.

The cross is there to call people to come to him. It cannot be denied and it cannot be evaded. The objective is that men and women are brought to

God through the forgiveness of their sins and the impartation of the life of the resurrected Son of God.

Consider then the cross, and neglect it at your peril. It stands in the way of hell-bound sinners. It should halt them in their waywardness, stop their slide and cause them to think earnestly of facing the consequences of their sin. God's great gift of his Son bearing their sin on the cross is a huge incentive and motivation to turn from their wicked ways and embrace his offer of forgiveness and life.

THE CHARACTER OF CHRIST

God said, 'This is My beloved Son, in whom I am well pleased' (Matt. 17:5); 'those who are in the flesh cannot please God' (Rom. 8:8). It is Christ who pleases God. Mankind has fallen away from him and is in a sinful state, so cannot please God. The only way in which we can please God is to have the life of Christ within us and expressing itself through us. His life, thus manifested, is then acceptable and pleasing to God. It is therefore logical and evident that Christ must dwell within us if we would have God's favour.

The meaning of the new birth

IT IS A BIBLICAL EXPERIENCE

Jesus spoke of the necessity of the new birth in John 3, John speaks clearly of it in his first epistle, Peter speaks of it (1 Peter 1:23) and James speaks of it (1:18). Paul speaks of the transformed character in Christ and exults in the use of several terms indicating the indwelling Christ. He speaks of our bodies as the temples of the Holy Spirit who dwells in us (1 Cor. 3:16). He says that by the Spirit of adoption we are able to cry, 'Abba, Father' (Rom. 8:15). The new birth is certainly biblical.

IT IS A DEFINITE EXPERIENCE

When a baby is born, it is a definite experience; similarly, when someone is born into the family of God, that too is a definite experience. The believer leaves the old paths and delights in new ones; he or she is inwardly transformed by the infusion of divine life. It cannot be anything other than a definite experience. We become new in Christ: old things have passed away and all things have become new. It is a great change wrought in the soul by the incoming Holy Spirit and, as such, is renewing in spirit and transforming in behaviour.

IT IS AN INSTANTANEOUS EXPERIENCE

Berkhof says, '[The new birth] is not a gradual process like sanctification, but is completed in a moment of time.'[27] Turner agrees: 'It takes place in a moment's time. There may be a long experience leading up to it, and the realization of it may not dawn upon the individual at once, but the experience itself is instantaneous. The very moment the divine Spirit comes into the heart, that very moment the individual is born again.'[28] It is a crisis with a view to a process when the life is to be lived in holiness and righteousness.

IT IS A MYSTERIOUS EXPERIENCE

The new birth is wrought in the heart of the believer and perceived only in the change in the inner condition of the heart and in its effects. 'The wind blows where it wishes, and you hear the sound of it, but cannot tell where it comes from and where it goes. So is everyone who is born of the Spirit' (John 3:8). It is a sovereign work—'The wind blows where it wishes'; it is a secret work—we 'cannot tell where it comes from and where it goes'; and it is a self-evident work—'you hear the sound of it'. We cannot account for the direction of the wind or for the beginning or extent of its influence. The wind blows—and we know that it is blowing, for we sense and feel it—but it is mysterious and incomprehensible.

Ezekiel cried to the wind to 'breathe on these slain' (Ezek. 37:9), and they stood to their feet, a mighty army. In the Song of Solomon, the Shulamite cries, 'Awake, O north wind, and come, O south! Blow upon my garden, that its spices may flow out' (4:16). On the day of Pentecost, 'suddenly there came a sound from heaven, as of a rushing mighty wind, and it filled the whole house where they were sitting' (Acts 2:2).

Wind illustrates the mystery of the work of the Spirit in his gracious operations. He is inexplicable and moves in the hearts of men mysteriously, tenderly, powerfully and savingly.

IT IS A BIRTH

Hastings declares, 'The new birth is the commencement of a new life ... As life commences in the child at the moment of its birth, so life commences in the soul when it is born again of the Spirit. The new birth is not merely a change of habit in a living soul, it is the commencement of life where there was none before.'[29]

God the Father is he 'who begot' and the believer is 'begotten of Him' (1 John 5:1) and 'born of the Spirit' (John 3:6). We who believe receive the Spirit and are born into the family of God. As members of God's family, and as God's children, we are 'heirs of God' (Rom. 8:17) and will therefore inherit the home of God, that is, heaven.

My wife and I have three children. When they were small, after having played outside with their friends they would all rush into the kitchen, chattering excitedly, panting and pushing one another, demanding orange juice and biscuits. Mummy would happily oblige and, with the noses of some of them barely above the table top, they would stretch across for their sweets. All the children were enjoying the benefits of the home, but not all of them will inherit our goods and our home when we die. Why not? Because they are not all our children and do not have our life. Only our children will inherit our home and possessions because they have our life. They are part of us.

God 'makes His sun rise on the evil and on the good, and sends rain on the just and on the unjust' (Matt. 5:45). Everyone enjoys the benefits of God's goodness here on earth, but not all will inherit God's home or his heaven. Why not? Because they do not have his life and are consequently not his spiritual children; 'flesh and blood cannot inherit the kingdom of God' (1 Cor. 15:50). A spiritual birth is a logical necessity. Without being born of the Spirit, it is simply not possible to enter into a spiritual heaven. 'That which is born of the flesh is flesh, and that which is born of the Spirit is spirit' (John 3:6).

If a goat wanted to become a lion, it would be no good for it to attempt to walk like a lion, roar like a lion or mix with lions in order to make them think that it was a lion. Even if it covered itself with an old lion skin and looked like a lion, it would still be a goat! The only way in which it could be a lion would be to be born a lion. It is therefore logical that, for people who want to be Christians, to walk as Christians walk, to speak as Christians speak, to mix with Christians in their churches and even to dress as Christians dress will not make them Christians. They must be born Christians! That is the only way in which they can become Christians and then inherit a spiritual home—heaven. Without the new birth, there is no spiritual change. Without a spiritual change, there is no heaven!

A SPIRITUAL EXPERIENCE

The new birth is the impartation of divine life. We become 'partakers of the divine nature' (2 Peter 1:4).

In the natural world we have three kingdoms: the mineral, plant and animal kingdoms. They are distinct from one another and there are great gulfs fixed between them. Now we are told that there is another kingdom, a spiritual kingdom, and to be part of it, we must be born into it. We must be born of the Spirit.

Regeneration is the divine act which imparts to the penitent believer spiritual life in personal union with Christ. It is the mighty Spirit coming into the life of the individual to enlighten, convince, strengthen, quicken and save. No ability of man can bring this about. No religious rite or activity, no moral reformation can effect this great and mighty change. It is wholly God's work and he performs it by his Spirit as he comes to live in and through the life of the believer.

Paul is very explicit in his explanation of the change; he says, 'God has sent forth the Spirit of His Son into your hearts, crying out, "Abba, Father!" Therefore you are no longer a slave but a son, and if a son, then an heir of God though Christ' (Gal. 4:6–7). So, to be a son (a child) of God, we must have the Spirit of his Son in our hearts; we must have the indwelling Christ. Paul claims that 'it is no longer I who live, but Christ lives in me' (Gal. 2:20). It is God in me! It is deity indwelling humanity! Nothing less than that! A Christian is in this sense a supernatural being, having been transferred from death to life and having the resurrected life of Jesus living in him or her by the Spirit. How utterly marvellous! What an enormous miracle of divine grace! We are citizens of heaven! We who refused to have this Man rule over us now have him within us giving us eternal life, for 'He who has the Son has life' (1 John 5:12).

IT IS A CREATION

The Lord who created man at the beginning, breathing into his nostrils the breath of life, recreates him by the operation of the Holy Spirit. 'There comes through the creative act of the Holy Spirit, a participation in the life of Christ,' says Lockyer.[30] The practical consequence is a radical change in the individual's character, desires and purposes.

'Therefore, if anyone is in Christ, he is a new creation; old things have passed away; behold, all things have become new' (2 Cor. 5:17). There is a complete revolution. The change is so radical that it is possible to speak of a new creature: 'For in Christ Jesus neither circumcision nor uncircumcision avails anything, but a new creation' (Gal. 6:15). Paul speaks of 'the new man which was created according to God, in true righteousness and holiness' (Eph. 4:24); and of the 'new man who is renewed in knowledge according to the image of Him who created him' (Col. 3:10).

The new man is thus renewed in the knowledge of God and is living in righteousness and holiness. Old things and sinful involvements are gone. He is truly a new creation.

IT IS A KNOWABLE EXPERIENCE

He lives! He lives within my heart; I know it to be true! I have the joy and assurance that he is within me and is guiding me onwards in his purposes. Duewel asks,

Is it possible for a dead person to become alive and well and not know it? Is it possible for a child to be born but there be no evidence of it? How could an adopted son make use of his rights as a son if he did not know for certain that he was a son? How could condemnation be gone if the person did not know he was forgiven (Rom. 8:1)? How could we have peace with God if we did not know we were justified and still feel guilty (Rom. 5:1)?[31]

The Christian has immense certainty and experiences the sheer joy of those who have come into a saving knowledge of Jesus through the great doctrines of the faith.

Conversely, if you don't know this certainty, it is just possible that you have never experienced it, that you have never been born again; for joy and glad assurance simply flow from that great and mighty change, that living encounter with the resurrected Christ indwelling and enthroned.

The method of the new birth

If the new birth is so important, how, then, am I to be born again?

THE WORD OF GOD

The Word points to Christ. The Spirit then uses the written Word and applies the truths of Christ and his great work, recorded in the Word, to our situation, for our salvation. Faith is then generated by the Spirit of God in the Word of God and results in our trusting Christ alone for salvation. Gordon says, 'Regeneration is the communication of the divine nature to man by the operation of the Holy Spirit through the Word.'[32]

'So then faith comes by hearing, and hearing by the word of God' (Rom. 10:17). In Luke 8 we have the parable of the sower and the soils, where Jesus says, 'The seed is the word of God' (v. 11). The seed has first to fall into the soil in order to germinate. The new birth therefore cannot be anticipated and begin before natural birth or take place after death. The seed must fall into the soil; the Word must fall into the hearts of living people. Faith in the hearts of those people comes by hearing, and hearing by the Word of God.

'[We have] been born again, not of corruptible seed but incorruptible, through the word of God which lives and abides forever' (1 Peter 1:23); 'Of His own will He brought us forth by the word of truth' (AV: 'begat he us'; James 1:18); 'in Christ Jesus I have begotten you through the gospel' (1 Cor. 4:15).

The Word of God is therefore an indispensable agent in leading men and women to Christ. Without it, we would not know of his person and work, we would not know of God's plan of salvation and we would yet be in our sins. The Word instructs us concerning God, man, sin, Christ and salvation. By it, we learn that we can approach God through Christ and be saved. The Word is indispensable.

A series of meetings was once held in a large church in South Africa. A farmer who styled himself 'the wildest man in the whole area' was persuaded to attend. He had no interest in the things of God and poured scorn on them. But as he sat there in that full church, listening to the earnest preaching of the Word of God, the Spirit of God applied that Word and brought him under great conviction of sin. In the pew he lifted his heart to God, repented of his sin and trusted Christ for salvation. At the close of the meeting, he rose, turned to his friends and said, 'I'm converted.' Outside the church they laughed him to scorn, but he insisted that he had come to Christ while the minister preached. 'It will last but a few days,' jeered his friends. Years later, this man said to me, 'That was nine years ago, and Christ means more to me now than ever before. Their prophecy failed and I am still following him with all my heart.' The Word had done its work!

THE DEATH AND RESURRECTION OF JESUS CHRIST

'Blessed be the God and Father of our Lord Jesus Christ, who according to His abundant mercy has begotten us again to a living hope through the resurrection of Jesus Christ from the dead' (1 Peter 1:3). In dying, the Lord Jesus took away the sins of the believing soul. This is the negative aspect; this is where the abundant mercy is revealed; this is the purging of sin, the cleansing which prepares the soul for the coming of the Holy Spirit. Sin must be dealt with in order for the soul to be transformed, and this is accomplished by Christ's death.

But he rose from the dead! He lives! We are born again to a living hope by that resurrected life of Christ which lives in the believer through faith. Christianity is the only religion which exists in the very life of its founder. Never would it be said of Muslims or Buddhists that they live in the lives of their founders or that their founders live in them. But this is the glory of Christianity: our God and Saviour lives in us and we live in him. If he were still in the tomb there would be no Christianity. The Jesus movement would have been snuffed out in the first few moments of its attempted existence. But he rose from the dead, and by that resurrected life, we live. Christianity glories in the empty tomb. Jesus lives in the lives of all those who welcome him into their hearts. By his life they are born again!

A minister friend of mine walked to his front door and his little son rushed after him, grabbing at his trousers. 'Daddy, where are you going?' he asked accusingly.

'Daddy is going to tell a lady how to open her heart to the Lord Jesus,' answered my friend.

'But doesn't she know?' asked the little boy.

'You tell Daddy how it is done,' said the father.

The little boy looked up at his daddy and said simply, 'You just open it.'

So simple, so profound, so life-transforming, so marvellous. And when we open them, the patient, persistent Saviour comes into our poor hearts and makes them his home. We are born of his Spirit.

THE HOLY SPIRIT

'[N]ot by works of righteousness which we have done, but according to His mercy He saved us, through the washing of regeneration and renewing of the Holy Spirit' (Titus 3:5); 'The Spirit Himself bears witness with our spirit that we are children of God' (Rom. 8:16).

'God is Spirit' (John 4:24). This is one of the great statements in Scripture concerning the nature of God. The Spirit of God renews our spirits and, through his mercy and grace, indwells us, bearing witness with our spirits that we are his children.

RECEIVING CHRIST

'But as many as received Him, to them He gave the right to become children of God, to those who believe in His name: who were born, not of blood, nor of the will of the flesh, nor of the will of man, but of God' (John 1:12–13). Who were born of God? Those who received him. Those, and only those!

You may have the trappings of religion, you may be up to your neck in church activities, you may even be a minister or Christian worker; but if you have not received Jesus Christ into your heart and life, you are not born of God and you are not saved.

God gave his Son as his unspeakable gift to mankind: 'For God so loved the world that He gave His only begotten Son' (John 3:16); 'as many as received Him' became his children and were born of him (John 1:12–13); 'He who has the Son has life' (1 John 5:12). In these three texts we see that the gift of Jesus is for us and that, as we take that gift by faith, we are born of God and we have the Son living within us. We have his eternal life.

If I held out a pen to you and said, 'I am giving you this pen; it is for you', what would you have to do to possess it? You would simply come forward and take the pen from my hand, and you would then naturally thank me. If you saw the pen and heard the words but did not come forward to take it from me, the loss would be yours. You would not possess that which was offered to you.

God gives us the tremendous gift of his Son: 'as many as received Him, to them He gave the right to become children of God', and these who received him were 'born … of God'. No one other than those who received him! How utterly important it is to receive him, for without receiving him, we are without his life and are lost for ever.

SAVING FAITH

'Whoever believes that Jesus is the Christ is born of God' (1 John 5:1); 'For you are all sons of God through faith in Christ Jesus' (Gal. 3:26). Christ is the anointed prophet, priest and king: he is the anointed prophet speaking God's word to the people; he is the anointed priest, making the supreme sacrifice to reconcile man to God; he is the anointed king over all those who are brought savingly into his kingdom. It was as Saviour that God 'anointed Jesus of Nazareth with the Holy Spirit' (Acts 10:38), and it is this Saviour in whom we are to believe.

Saving faith is not an intellectual acceptance of truth, for: 'Even the demons believe—and tremble!' (James 2:19); it is not something which we understand and with which we are familiar; it is not merely head knowledge. It is more than that: it is a heart acceptance; it is a trust in, a relying upon, a clinging to the fact that Jesus is my own personal Saviour. All those who trust in and rest upon the fact that this great Saviour is *their* Saviour are born of God.

We can know all about God's plan of salvation yet not receive Christ or trust him to save us. Similarly, we can stand on one side of a great bridge and know that it will hold our weight if we begin walking across it, but unless we trust ourselves to the bridge and begin walking over it, we will remain on the same side; we will not get to the other side! The great bridge is Jesus. In him we are to trust, finding that he is able to take us right across the divide. Trust yourself to him and put your faith into action. Trust, believe, be born again!

The necessity of the new birth

Jesus said, 'Most assuredly, I say to you, unless one is born again, he cannot see the kingdom of God ... You must be born again' (John 3:3,7).

THE COMMAND IS IMPARTIAL

Jesus made no distinction; there was no special choice. He said 'unless one is born again ... ' He did not specify the type or nature of that person who is to be born again. He does not require super intelligence, blameless morality or dedicated religiosity before a person is born again. He states categorically that 'unless one is born again, he cannot see the kingdom of God'—anyone, good or bad, religious or irreligious, just anyone! God is no respecter of persons. The command comes to all, irrespective of rank or position.

You could be rich or poor; the command comes to you: 'You must be born again.' You could be well known or unknown: you too must be born again. You may move in high or low social circles: you must be born again. You may or may not have an attractive personality with a large circle of friends: you must be born again. You may be old or young, black or white, Roman Catholic, Protestant or anything else: you must be born again. You may be immersed in trouble or enjoying an easy life: you must be born again. You may be a young man, full of hope and ambition with the world at your feet: you must be born again. You may be a young woman, beautiful, attractive, loving life: you must be born again. You may have a beautiful relationship with your spouse; don't let that hold you back for fear of disturbing the relationship: you must be born again. You may be in a group from which it would be difficult to break free: you must be born again. You may be someone who attends church regularly: you must be born again. You may be full of good works, helping wherever you can: you must be born again. Whoever you are: you must be born again! 'For there is no partiality with God' (Rom. 2:11).

A young businessman who was an earnest Christian lay dying in a state of delirium. A close friend came to his bedside and leant over him. 'John,' he said, 'John, do you know me?'

John looked at him for a moment and then said, 'No, I don't know you, but whoever you are, you must be born again.' His consuming passion for the lost held true right to the end of his life.

THE COMMAND IS IMPERATIVE

There is no other way—no way but the new birth! No other way to get into heaven; no other way to be with God for ever. Don't kid yourself: religion is not enough. It is only the new birth that is sufficient. Jesus said, 'I am the way, the truth, and the life. No one comes to the Father except through Me' (John 14:6); 'I am the door. If anyone enters by Me, he will be saved' (John 10:9). 'Nor is there salvation in any other, for there is no other name under heaven given among men by which we must be saved' (Acts 4:12). Jesus said that anything other than the new birth is insufficient and your soul will be lost—lost for ever!

Spurgeon often preached on the new birth. The story is told that, after one meeting, a lady said to him, 'Mr Spurgeon, I am tired of you always preaching on this subject. Why do you always say, "You must be born again"?'

'Because, madam,' answered Spurgeon, 'you must be born again!'

Once when I was in Toronto, I was shown a church and told how godly bishop John Taylor Smith once preached there on the new birth and, at the end of his sermon, pointed to the archdeacon in the church. He said, 'Nothing can replace the new birth. You could be an archdeacon like my friend over there and not be born again. You must be born again.'

The next day, the bishop received a letter from the archdeacon in which he wrote, 'My dear bishop, you have found me out. I never knew the joy of which Christians speak. I have been preaching for twenty-seven years. Mine has been hard, cold, legal service. But when you pointed at me and said "You must be born again", I knew that I had never been born again. Can you help me?'

Yes, the bishop could help him, and after two hours of conversation, the archdeacon took his place as a sinner in need of God's salvation and trusted Christ to come into his heart and make him a true born-again Christian. Are you born again? Are you?

The moment of the new birth

'Whoever believes that Jesus is the Christ is born of God' (1 John 5:1). When we respond to his loving call, when we repent of our pointless attempts to attain salvation in our own strength, when we open our hearts to his gracious movings, when we place our faith in Jesus as our personal Saviour, when we trust him to come into our lives and save us, at that moment we are born again. The moment that faith is exercised the miracle takes place.

I had been under conviction of sin for months when I returned home from boarding school for a free weekend. Together with my family, I attended a series of meetings held in the nearby village. One night, as a fifteen-year-old lad, I responded to the appeal of the gospel and, sitting on an old bench in a country hall, I gave my heart to Jesus and asked him to forgive my sins and to come into my life. I walked into that hall a child of darkness; I walked out a child of light. I walked in without Christ; I walked out with Christ in my heart. I walked in unsaved; I walked out saved by divine mercy and sovereign grace. The transformation took place in just a few brief words of confession, commitment and faith. Jesus had come into my heart and life and I was saved! I was born again! My life was changed for ever and my future was secure in him. Assurance welled up in my heart and I knew that I had begun a new life in God. Praise his name!

Notes

1 **Louis Berkhof,** *Manual of Christian Doctrine* (Grand Rapids, MI: Eerdmans, 1933), p. 236.

2 **Robert Candlish,** *1 John* (London: Banner of Truth, 1973), p. 270.

3 *The Salvation Army Handbook of Doctrine* (London: Salvation Army Headquarters, 1927), p. 103.

4 H. Burkhardt in **Sinclair B. Ferguson, David F. Wright, J. I. Packer** (eds.), *New Dictionary of Theology* (Leicester: IVP, 1988), p. 574.

5 **Alban Douglas,** *One Hundred Bible Lessons* (Manila: OMF, 1966), p. 119.

6 **Wesley L. Duewel,** *God's Great Salvation* (Greenwood, IN: OMS International, 1991), pp. 125,153.

7 **William Evans,** *The Great Doctrines of the Bible* (1912; 1972, Chicago: Moody Press), p. 151.

8 **E. F. Kevan,** *Salvation* (Welwyn: Evangelical Press, 1973), p. 61.

9 **Herbert Lockyer,** *All the Doctrines of the Bible* (Grand Rapids, MI: Zondervan, 1964), pp. 177,180.

10 **John L. Nuelson** in **J. Orr** (ed.), *International Standard Bible Encyclopedia*, vol. iv (Grand Rapids, MI: Eerdmans, 1976), pp. 2548, 2550.

11 **Robert Lee,** *Doctrinal Outlines* (London: Pickering & Inglis, n.d.), p. 109.

12 **J. I. Packer** in **W. A. Elwell** (ed.), *Evangelical Dictionary of Theology* (Basingstoke: Marshall Pickering, 1984), p. 924.

13 **Myer Pearlman,** *Knowing the Doctrines of the Bible* (Springfield, MO: Gospel Publishing House, 1937), p. 242.

14 **A. H. Strong,** *Systematic Theology* (London: Pickering & Inglis, 1907), p. 809.

15 **Harold B. Kuhn** in **Richard Taylor** (ed.), *Beacon Dictionary of Theology* (Kansas City, MO: Beacon Hill, 1983), p. 445.

16 **Henry C. Thiessen,** *Systematic Theology* (Grand Rapids, MI: Eerdmans, 1979), p. 279.

17 **R. A. Torrey,** *What the Bible Teaches* (London: James Nisbet & Co., n.d.), pp. 324,327.

18 **Orton Wiley,** *Introduction to Christian Theology* (Kansas City, MO: Beacon Hill, 1963), p. 284.

19 **Ernest S. Williams,** *Systematic Theology*, vol. ii (Springfield, MO: Gospel Publishing House, 1953), p. 238.

20 **William Barclay,** *The Letters of John and Jude* (Edinburgh: St Andrew Press, 1958), p. 85.

21 **Simon J. Kistemaker,** *James and 1–3 John* (Welwyn: Evangelical Press, 1986), p. 289.

22 **John Stott,** *The Epistles of John: An Introduction and Commentary* (Tyndale New Testament Commentaries; London: The Tyndale Press, 1964), p. 116.

23 **F. F. Bruce,** *The Epistles of John* (London: Pickering & Inglis, 1970), p. 95.

24 **Stott,** *Epistles of John*, p. 161.

25 Ibid. p. 174.

26 **W. Hendriksen,** *Gospel of John* (New Testament Commentary; Grand Rapids, MI: Baker, 1954), p. 134.

27 Berkhof, *Manual of Christian Doctrine*, p. 237.

28 J. Clyde Turner, *Soul-winning Doctrines* (Nashville, TN: Southern Baptist, 1943), p. 25.

29 J. Hastings, *Great Texts of the Bible* (Edinburgh: T & T Clark, 1912), p. 170.

30 Lockyer, *All the Doctrines of the Bible*, p. 180.

31 Duewel, *God's Great Salvation*, p. 129.

32 A. J. Gordon, 'Two-Fold Life', in **Strong,** *Systematic Theology*, p. 824.

Assurance: the witness of the Spirit

Definitions of assurance

- 'Scripture clearly holds out to every Christian the privilege of knowing that he is a child of God. The Spirit uses Scripture to bring us assurance of salvation' (Bruce Milne).[1]
- 'Christian Assurance is not an expression of human optimism or presumption, but a persuasion from God' (*The New Bible Dictionary*).[2]
- 'The testimony of the Spirit is superior to reason. For as God alone can properly bear witness to his own words, so these words will not obtain full credibility in the hearts of men, until they are sealed by the inward witness of the Spirit' (John Calvin).[3]
- 'There is the assurance of grace and salvation which consists in a sense of security and safety, rising in many instances to the height of an "assured conviction that the individual believer has had his sins pardoned and his soul saved"' (Louis Berkhof).[4]
- 'There is an inner witness, a feeling, a sense within, produced by the Spirit of God who dwells within you, that you are a part of the great family of God' (Ray Stedman).[5]
- 'When John says "that ye may know that ye have eternal life" … it is not a matter of inference and deduction but a matter of revelation from God' (C. H. Spurgeon).[6]
- 'The felt presence of Christ in our hearts (1 John 3:24) assures us that we are in the way of life leading to endless glory' (J. Agar Beet).[7]
- 'The Word of God appears to me to teach that a believer may arrive at an assured confidence with regard to his own salvation' (J. C. Ryle).[8]
- 'Assurance is not a formal acceptance of doctrine, but a vital certainty, incorporated into the Christian life' (*Zondervan's Pictorial Bible Dictionary*).[9]

- 'With the Spirit making us new creatures in Christ Jesus comes the consciousness of our sonship … [W]ith this comes the peace of conscience … and confidence towards God' (Ernest S. Williams).[10]
- 'The New Testament stresses the normative character of assurance, portraying Christian faith as joyful confidence in Jesus Christ. Paul grounds assurance in the purpose of God, the saving work of Christ, and the ministry of the Spirit, against which nothing can prevail' (*New Dictionary of Theology*).[11]
- 'The Bible lays down very clearly that it is perfectly normal for a Christian to be assured of his own salvation. In fact it is difficult to find in either the OT or the NT any instance of a child of God doubting whether he/she is a child of God' (D. MacLeod).[12]
- 'The indwelling life puts forth a confident utterance' (D. D. Whedon).[13]

The necessity of assurance

How utterly essential it is to have assurance of salvation! How absurd to fight it!

- Without assurance there is no joy, but often nagging doubts and fears.
- Without assurance we have no confidence to witness to others about the Lord, for we are not sure that we know him ourselves.
- Without assurance we do not extend the work of God, for we cannot speak with confidence of something of which we are not sure.
- Without assurance we fail to serve the Lord effectively.
- Without assurance it is difficult to attempt to grow in grace.
- Without assurance our worship has no wholehearted devotion nor thrill of commitment.
- Without assurance we fail to enjoy our salvation and do not have the joy of fellowship with God.
- Without assurance we are kept in a constant state of anxiety and sorrow of heart, wondering if we will ever make it to God's heaven.
- Without assurance we fail to enjoy open-hearted fellowship with those who do have assurance, and we cannot enter into stimulating fellowship with them, for we feel we are outside their company.

ASSURANCE DENIED

Amazingly, the lack of assurance in strongly Reformed areas such as the north-west of Scotland and parts of Holland has been almost cultivated and encouraged. It is thought that to claim that you are sure of your salvation is a mark of pride, and to admit that you do not have assurance is a mark of humility. In fact, if you say that you have assurance, your testimony will be suspect. It is necessary to have plaguing doubts, for you are a mere mortal and can make a mistake. Only God knows whether you are his, and you are to trust in his electing purposes, apply the means of grace, live as the Bible teaches you to live and hope that you will be gathered into his kingdom at the end of your life. It is expected that you must have doubts. That is part and parcel of the faith!

I well remember a young Christian coming to visit my Scottish father-in-law. They were speaking enthusiastically of the things of God, but I thought that I had better find out where Graham stood spiritually, so I asked him, 'Graham, are you saved? Do you know the Lord?'

His face fell as he answered, 'Oh, well, I can't say that now. When I first began to follow the Lord, I had that assurance, but they came from the church and told me not to be so presumptuous. Only God knows who are his, and I shouldn't speak so confidently about the Lord.'

I was amazed at this reasoning but realized that those in this doctrinal rut were seriously damaging the cause of Christ. Theological complexities lead on to a hurtful, heartbreaking confusion.

Why, the very *Westminster Shorter Catechism*, with which Scottish children were raised, tells us of the necessity of this assurance! It says, 'The benefits which in this life do accompany or flow from justification, adoption, and sanctification, are, assurance of God's love, peace of conscience, joy in the Holy Ghost, increase of grace, and perseverance therein to the end.'[14] Assurance of God's love! The human heart can never be at rest while in doubt. Opinions, beliefs, reasonings, authority of men, all fail to calm the fears and assure the sinner of salvation. So we have uncertain and despondent penitents! Only the full assurance of faith will give perfect peace to the penitent sinner.

God wants us to be sure that he loves us, that he is our loving heavenly

Father, that he brings comfort and peace and gives us the joy of knowing him. To go against this is to deny the teaching of the Catechism and, much more importantly, the Bible itself. It is a false premise and wrong theology. In fact, it is heresy to say that a child of God cannot have assurance of salvation. The Holy Spirit witnesses to the fact of assurance in the hearts of those who trust him for salvation.

FALSE ASSURANCE

On the other hand, there are those who base their supposed assurance on very flimsy evidence which will not stand up to scriptural scrutiny.

After counselling and prayer, soul-winners say to seekers, 'Don't you feel better now?' Of course the seekers feel better. They have confessed their sins and that is a load off their consciences. The seekers are honestly trying to do their duty and go in the right direction—that also makes them feel better, but it is no proof of their having found the Lord. A large number of seekers stop right there. They are deceived into thinking that this easing of conscience is proof of their conversion; that it is the witness of the Spirit in their hearts.

They pray, read the Bible and go to church, trusting, even without knowing it, in their own ability to keep themselves, but in a little while they get discouraged and turn away from it all. They are said to have 'backslidden', but in reality, even though they were counselled, they were never converted in the first place. Their foundations were false and their confidence and assurance inadequate to meet life or eternity. Some become hardened and bitter sceptics, far more difficult to reach than ever before. Others keep on for some time with outward formalities but with no inward assurance, and their enjoyment of the Christian life is limited to social engagements with those whom they meet in their church activities. Theirs is legal service. They become nominal and ineffective 'Christians', having a form of godliness but denying the power thereof. Their Christianity is simply an empty shell.

Intellectual assent to a spiritual truth is now substituted for confidence in a personal Saviour which should be expressed in utter abandonment to him. They rest on mere statements which they have intellectually accepted, and not upon the life-transforming faith transaction based on God's Word and applied by God's Spirit.

It is the Holy Spirit alone who witnesses in the heart to the incoming Spirit—and that assurance is not presumption but sheer joy in the One who brings his own inner witness. He sets the joy-bells ringing and sweeps away the doubts by his very presence. It is not the exhortation from the counsellor but the wonderful presence of God which gives the glad assurance of salvation from heaven itself when a sinner trusts the Saviour.

HISTORICAL WITNESS

At the dawning of the Reformation period in the early sixteenth century, the joy of the felt presence of God dwelling in the believer was heralded by the Reformers. Luther asserted, 'Faith is a living, deliberate confidence in the grace of God, so certain that for it one could die a thousand deaths, and such confidence and knowledge of divine grace makes us joyous, intrepid and cheerful towards God and all creation.'[15] The eminent Anglican churchman Richard Hooker testified, 'The Spirit of God hath been given to us to assure us that we are sons of God, to embolden us to call upon him as our Father.'[16] Samuel Wesley, the father of John and Charles, said as he lay dying, 'the inward witness, this is the strongest proof of Christianity'.[17] George Whitefield was a strong proponent of the inner witness. He said,

I will not say that all our letter-learned preachers deny this doctrine in express words, but they do, however, in effect. For they talk openly against inward feelings, and say that we may have God's Spirit without feeling it. [This], in reality, is to deny the thing itself. And if I had a mind to hinder the progress of the gospel, and to establish the kingdom of darkness, I would go around telling people [that] they may have the Spirit of God and yet not feel it.[18]

The saintly John Owen speaks of 'the Comforter who, by a word of promise, or otherwise, overpowers the heart with a comfortable persuasion ... that [the believer] is a child of God'.[19]

John Wesley actually selected the witness of the Spirit as 'the main doctrine of the Methodists'.[20] H. B. Workman, Principal of Westminster College, London, from 1903–1930, claimed that the doctrine of assurance 'was the fundamental contribution of Methodism to the life and thought of the Church'.[21] This does not mean that the doctrine was peculiar to Methodism, but the Wesleys and Whitefield reasserted it at a time when it was regarded as a dangerous innovation. The witness of the Spirit is now conceded to be the privilege of sonship, but it was the teaching at the time of the eighteenth-century revival which made it come alive to the people. The preachers acknowledged their debt concerning the Spirit's witness to the Puritans and the Moravians, but all would trace their origins to the Word of God.

The witness is scriptural

THE FACT OF ASSURANCE
The Bible is very clear throughout that those who belong to God are assured of their relationship with him. This assurance is not experienced by coercion, persuasion or supposed invention, nor is it hopeful expectation or of human derivation. It is experienced by divine impartation. God gives the witness of the Spirit in the heart, and those who are his know that fact by virtue of the Spirit who witnesses within.

Where do we find in either Old or New Testament anyone who doubted his or her salvation? We look in vain. The Psalms especially breathe assurance. The psalmist knows that this God is his God: 'The LORD is my shepherd,' he gratefully acknowledges (Ps. 23:1). Job says, 'Though He slay me, yet will I trust Him' (13:15) and 'I know that my Redeemer lives' (19:25). This is very personal and blessedly reassuring.

WITNESSING
The New Testament throbs with vibrant hope and joyful certainty. In the book of Acts, the boldness and confidence with which the believers witnessed speak of a deep conscious, inward assurance. They were in no doubt about the abiding presence of God, and therefore spoke with the ring of authority.

Paul's testimony before Agrippa in Acts 26 is full of assurance and challenge, so much so that Agrippa cries out, 'You almost persuade me to become a Christian' (v. 28). Paul's bold certainty produced effective evangelistic activity. If he had not been certain of what he believed and experienced, his words would have had little effect and his testimony and presentation would have failed—but he was sure!

PREACHING
The preaching in the New Testament is full of vital assurances. Consider:
- Peter at Pentecost: 'this is what was spoken by the prophet Joel' (Acts 2:16);
- Stephen: 'Look! I see the heavens opened and the Son of Man standing at the right hand of God!' (Acts 7:56);
- Paul at Antioch: 'through this Man is preached to you the forgiveness of sins; and by Him everyone who believes is justified from all things' (Acts 13:38–39);
- Paul at Athens: 'the One whom you worship without knowing, Him I proclaim to you' (Acts 17:23).

TEACHING
The teaching of the New Testament is also full of assurance. The writers are sure of their message. They speak with no uncertain sound. Their experience with God has burned the message into mind and heart and there is the ring of joy and assurance. The word 'know' occurs over thirty times in John's first epistle, which contains just over 100 verses. It is full of assurance.
A few examples may suffice to illustrate:
- Peter: 'by which have been given to us exceedingly great and precious promises, that through these you may be partakers of the divine nature' (2 Peter 1:4);
- Jude: 'Now to Him who is able to keep you from stumbling' (Jude 24);
- Paul: 'the full assurance of understanding' (Col. 2:2); 'For our gospel [came] … in much assurance' (1 Thes. 1:5);
- John: 'He who has the Son has life' (1 John 5:12); 'that you may know that you have eternal life' (1 John 5:13);

- The writer to the Hebrews: 'the full assurance of hope' (Heb. 6:11); 'let us draw near with a true heart in full assurance of faith' (Heb. 10:22).

The gospel comes in 'much assurance' and in the 'full assurance' of 'understanding', 'hope' and 'faith'. We certainly have assurance in abundance throughout the New Testament.

THE MEANS OF ASSURANCE

Who imparts the inward knowledge? By what means do we have this personal assurance?

John answers, 'And by this we know that He abides in us, by the Spirit whom He has given us' (1 John 3:24); 'By this we know that we abide in Him, and He in us, because He has given us of His Spirit' (1 John 4:13); 'it is the Spirit who bears witness, because the Spirit is truth' (1 John 5:6).

Paul affirms, 'The Spirit Himself bears witness with our spirit that we are children of God' (Rom. 8:16).

There is no question: the testimony is given by the Spirit of God to our spirits. He testifies within our souls. It is the authentic witness of the Spirit apart from any mode or rite. It is conveyed direct from Spirit to spirit. Wesley says, 'It is given immediately by the power of the Holy Ghost, and what none can have for another, but for himself only.'[22] It is the direct operation of the Spirit of God upon the heart and mind of man.

THE FOCUS OF ASSURANCE

The Spirit of God brings the assurance to our hearts but the assurance focuses on the Lord Jesus Christ: 'whoever calls on the name of the LORD shall be saved' (Acts 2:21); 'through this Man is preached to you the forgiveness of sins' (Acts 13:38); 'Who shall separate us from the love of Christ?' (Rom. 8:35); 'I ... [have] a desire to depart and be with Christ' (Phil. 1:23); 'I know whom I have believed and am persuaded that He is able to keep what I have committed to Him until that Day' (2 Tim. 1:12); 'by this we know that we know Him, if we keep His commandments' (1 John 2:3). The redeemed soul finds that Jesus is living within and his presence brings reality to the whole transaction. It is Jesus who is exalted by the Spirit and who is revealed as the soul's personal Saviour. The witness centres in and focuses upon the Lord Jesus, the glorious Saviour.

THE SCOPE OF THE ASSURANCE

Spiritual truths are spiritually discerned. The natural man cannot reason his way to God. The philosopher who speaks of the Supreme Being is but a refined idolater who worships his or her own intellectual creation. Those who enjoy the inward witness of the Spirit have a knowledge of spiritual truth which can be acquired in no other way. Spiritual truth comes, not through natural reasoning or human understanding, but through divine revelation imparted by the Spirit. Spiritual truth is not mentally acquired but spiritually revealed. We do not grasp spiritual things by mental comprehension only, but by spiritual appropriation. Truths are only discovered and known by an inward witness. Let us look at a few of these truths:

- Redemption: 'knowing that you were not redeemed with corruptible things, like silver or gold ... but with the precious blood of Christ, as of a lamb without blemish and without spot' (1 Peter 1:18–19). We can know that we are redeemed!
- Crucifixion: 'knowing this, that our old man was crucified with Him, that the body of sin might be done away with, that we should no longer be slaves of sin. For he who has died has been freed from sin' (Rom. 6:6–7). We can know that we are free and no longer remain under the bondage of sin.
- Confidence: 'I know whom I have believed and am persuaded that He is able to keep what I have committed to Him until that Day' (2 Tim. 1:12). We can know that our future is safe with him.
- Trust: 'And we know that all things work together for good to those who love God' (Rom. 8:28). Whatever happens to us as children of God, we can rest in him, for there is always a purpose—God's purpose.

John's first epistle has a wealth of wonderful teaching in this regard:
- We know that we know God (2:3).
- We know that we are in him (2:5).
- We know that it is the last hour (2:18).
- We know the truth (2:21).
- We know that when he shall appear, we shall be like him (3:2).
- We know that he was manifested to take away our sins (3:5).
- We know that we have passed from death to life (3:14).

- We know that we are of the truth (3:19).
- We know that Christ abides in us by the Spirit (3:24).
- We know that Jesus Christ is the Son of God (4:2).
- We know the spirit of truth and the spirit of error (4:6).
- We know that we abide in Christ (4:13).
- We know the love of God (4:16).
- We know that we love the children of God (5:2).
- We know that God answers prayer (5:15).
- We know that there is deliverance from sin (5:18).
- We know that we are of God (5:19).

What a wealth of spiritual knowledge here! This produces unshakeable convictions. This assurance gives power and authority to the believer to know without a doubt that he or she is a child of God and, further, to testify confidently and preach powerfully the wonderful truths of God's salvation.

The witness is direct

There is a difference between the direct witness to the soul and the indirect witness which is seen in the removal of the guilty conscience and the evidence of a transformed life. There are, then, both the direct and the indirect witnesses. First of all, we see concerning the direct witness that:

IT IS DEFINED

Wesley's definition given in a sermon in 1746 was exactly reproduced in 1767. It is as follows: 'The testimony of the Spirit is an inward impression on the soul, whereby the Spirit of God directly witnesses to my spirit, that I am a child of God, that Jesus Christ hath loved me, and given himself for me, and that all my sins are blotted out, and I, even I, am reconciled to God.'[23] He amplified this:

The Spirit itself bore witness to my spirit, that I was a child of God, gave me an evidence hereof; and I immediately cried 'Abba, Father'! And this I did (and so did you) before I reflected on or was conscious of, any fruit of the Spirit. It was from this testimony received, that love, joy, peace, and the whole fruit of the Spirit flowed. First I heard

'Thy sins are forgiven! Accepted thou art!'
I listen'd, and heaven sprang up in my heart.[24]

This is the testimony of the children of God worldwide. The Spirit of God witnesses with our sprits that the mighty change has taken place and that we, who were children of darkness, are now children of light. The mighty transaction has taken place and we are part of the body of Christ. We are no longer under condemnation but instead know that our sins have been forgiven. We are part of the family of God, and we know it! The Spirit witnesses to that wonderful truth. Our lives have been transformed by the power of the Spirit who witnesses within our hearts.

IT IS MYSTERIOUS

Wesley speaks of the Spirit's witness as a 'strong, though inexplicable operation'.[25] He says,

The manner how the divine testimony is manifested to the heart, I do not take upon me to explain … As no one knoweth the things of a man, save the spirit of a man that is in him; so the manner of the things of God knoweth no one, save the Spirit of God. But the fact we know; namely that the Spirit of God does give a believer such a testimony of his adoption, that while it is present to the soul, he can no more doubt the reality of his sonship, than he can doubt the shining of the sun, while he stands in the full blaze of his beams.[26]

This is something like the beauty of a sunset, the brightness of a star or the scent of a rose. They are indefinable. You sense the awe and beauty of the moment but find it difficult to describe. It must be experienced to be known. I once stood at the incomparable Victoria Falls in southern Africa. The water level was at the highest it had ever been. The Falls are one mile wide—simply a slit in the flat terrain—and the mighty Zambezi River pours over the edge into the chasm 360 feet below. Its roar could be heard for miles. Spray covered us, drenched us and soared above us, disappearing into the air while hundreds of rainbows flitted everywhere as we edged our way carefully along the wet surface. How do you describe that? It is an awesome experience! The only way to grasp the enormity and awe of the scene is to be there and sense for yourself the marvel of the 'smoke that thunders'. So it is with the witness of the Spirit. How do we describe it? We cannot. It is the inward knowledge that we are God's and that he has given to us his Son who now dwells in our hearts. He who has the Son has life!

IT IS USUALLY IMMEDIATE

Wesley says that the full assurance is 'wrought in the soul by the same immediate inspiration of the Holy Ghost, not an opinion, not a bare construction of Scripture [but as] given immediately by the power of the Holy Ghost'.[27] That needs clarification, for not everyone receives the witness at the moment of believing. Usually it is immediate and the soul is instantly strengthened and inspired by the assurance which is communicated Spirit to spirit, but on other occasions it may take a while before God seals the deal by his assuring presence. Sometimes we may simply have to continue to believe and trust that what we read in the Bible will be true, and is actually already true, in us. Then, sometimes slowly or sometimes suddenly, the realization dawns, and we know that we are his! It may take a day, a week or even longer, but when the Spirit witnesses within, we will certainly know.

IT IS NECESSARY FOR FULL ENJOYMENT OF SALVATION

It was at first thought by teachers in the eighteenth century that it would be well-nigh impossible that a person could be born again and not know it. Wesley said at one time that 'he who perceives it not, has it not'.[28] It seemed to them that a consciousness of acceptance was essential to justifying grace. In later years, Wesley modified his teaching to accommodate a few exceptions whom he felt might have been in favour with God but who went about mourning all the day, either because of bodily disorders or because of ignorance of the gospel promises.

Without a doubt, every believer may and ought to possess an assurance of salvation, but there will sadly always be those few unfortunates who have been pardoned and redeemed yet lack the assurance of salvation. Tragically, some are tormented by doubts for years when they could gain such assurance and joy by simply trusting the promises of God and knowing that they belong to the Lord. Let me illustrate:

If you were to go on a long journey but did not want to take a very precious jewel with you, you might come to me and ask me to keep it safe for you until you returned. I would lock it in the safe and off you would go. After going a fair distance, you might phone me and ask whether the jewel is still safe. 'Oh yes,' I would reply, 'you saw me locking it in the safe.' You would be relieved and would continue on your journey. Having gone a further distance, you might phone again and ask the same question: 'Is the jewel still safe?' 'Yes,' I would reply, 'it is still locked in the safe.' After some time you might phone again and ask the same question, to which I would now reply with amazement, 'Yes, it's in the safe!' If, after yet another while, you phone and ask the same question yet again, I would be justified in thinking that you did not trust my character or my word, and would say so: 'Don't you trust me? I told you that it is locked away. It is safe there!'

That is how we often treat God. We commit our lives to him and ask him to save us, yet we don't seem to trust him to do what he has said he will do. He said that 'the one who comes to Me I will by no means cast out' (John 6:37). That is his word! It cannot be broken! Have you come to him? Have you committed your life to him? Has he promised to keep that which is committed to him? Yes! Yes! Yes! Then don't doubt his word! Trust him that when you have asked him to forgive you, to cleanse you, to come into your heart as you give yourself to him, he will do what he says—otherwise it would appear that you are actually doubting his character! He is trustworthy! He will do what he says. You can safely trust his word and rest upon it for your salvation.

Has God said, 'Repent'? Have you obeyed? If you have acknowledged your sin and sincerely repented, you can answer, 'Yes.'

Has God said, 'Confess your sins'? If you have done that, you can again answer, 'Yes.' Has God said, 'Receive Jesus Christ'? Have you received him? If you have, you can answer, 'Yes.'

Has God said, 'Believe, trust'? If you have placed your trust in him, then stand firm. He will be true to his word. He cannot lie. His word is eternally true and you are basing your salvation on that unchangeable and impregnable word of the living God. The Spirit of God makes the word real in our hearts and that brings assurance to us!

The witness is indirect

Is the direct witness a safe test? Is it not possible to be deceived? Is it not dangerous?

If it were the only witness, it could be questionable, but to balance it we have a corrective or confirmative witness—the indirect witness. This has a threefold appeal:

THE APPEAL TO A CHANGED EXPERIENCE

The witness of the Spirit stems from that 'vast and mighty change' of regeneration.[29] If Almighty God has come to dwell in the soul of man, his life must manifest itself in distinctive ways. Those who do not show evidence of transformation cannot rightly claim assurance.

The Bible clearly states, 'if anyone is in Christ, he is a new creation; old things have passed away; behold, all things have become new' (2 Cor. 5:17). The truly regenerate discover manifestations of the new life within themselves. There are definite evidences of an inward and outward change. There is a 'humble joy' soon followed by 'meekness, patience, gentleness, longsuffering. There is a soft, yielding spirit; a mild sweetness, a tenderness of soul which words cannot express.'[30] This change confirms the direct witness of the Spirit and constitutes further grounds of assurance. False testimony produces just the opposite effect: such people become haughty and overbearing, and are unwilling to receive reproof.

THE APPEAL TO THE TESTIMONY OF SCRIPTURE

Dangers of self-deception come from the presumption of a natural mind and from the delusions of the devil. Those who are puffed up and rank themselves among Christians persuade themselves that they have the witness. The testimony must be tested by Scripture.

THE SOUL MUST HAVE REPENTED

Those who are self-deceived are strangers to biblical repentance. They have never known a broken and contrite heart. The remembrance of their sins has never been grievous to them, nor has 'the burden of them [become] intolerable'.[31] They may have repeated certain words of repentance, but they never meant what they said. Inwardly, they have never turned away from their old lives.

THE SOUL MUST HAVE BEEN BORN AGAIN

The deluded know no such change! This is language which they do not understand. They tell you that they were always Christians. If they have been brought up religiously, they see no need for any change. They might even have persuaded themselves that they are born again, although they understand it only vaguely. Yet if they gave themselves time to think and examine themselves, they would know that they are not born of the Spirit, that they have never known God, and that they have mistaken the voice of nature for the voice of God.

THE SOUL MUST SHOW THE FRUIT OF THE SPIRIT

New Testament writers set before us the evidences of a genuine spiritual experience. The tree is known by its fruit. These effects of the divine encounter must, of necessity, be present. John, in his first epistle, states some of the distinguishing marks of the new life in Christ. Here are a few:
- the practice of righteousness (2:29);
- victory over sin (3:9);
- love for fellow believers (4:7);
- acknowledgement of the Lordship of Christ (5:1);
- the overcoming of the world (5:4).

Other portions of Scripture give further evidences and, as we examine our experiences in the light of God's Word, we find that the promises and precepts act either as a confirmative upon the direct witness, assuring us of its genuineness, or as a corrective, revealing self-deception.

THE APPEAL TO COLLECTIVE EXPERIENCE

The individual experience must be checked and balanced by the collective experience of Christian people. Times of sharing in a Christian group are so important, as it is then that mutual spiritual aid and instruction can be given and where experiences can be assessed by others. This helps to eliminate false professions and folk can get alongside and pray with the one who is perhaps having a problem. It also saves from excess, as the collective experience of the group is a fairly safe haven in which to put your testimony to the test. Within a group there are normally wise, helpful and mature Christians who can guide and help those who need to be brought to a sure trust in God. The experiences of believers, the warmth and encouragement of their fellowship and the joy of sharing Christian truths and experiences provide a corrective or confirmative influence upon the direct witness.

The witness is beneficial

There are many real benefits from the Spirit's witness. Here are a few:

CERTAINTY CONCERNING THE FUNDAMENTAL DOCTRINES

It is the Holy Spirit who alone preserves orthodoxy. If a church loses the presence and power of the Holy Spirit, it will soon lose its doctrines. It will become worldly, doctrinally liberal and decadent. The message from its pulpit will become insipid and its people will cease to have vibrancy and glorious vitality in their lives and witness. It is the Spirit who gives conviction and confidence concerning the things that are fundamental to salvation and the Christian life. Where the Spirit's witness is strong, the Bible will be held as God's Word, and its doctrines will be avidly studied and joyfully believed. The great fundamentals of the faith, such as the authority of the Bible, the deity of Christ, the virgin birth, the atonement and the second coming, will be firmly believed and joyfully proclaimed. Where the Spirit has departed, the Bible will lose its importance, its doctrines will be doubted, denied and disbelieved, and the church will degenerate into a religious and social society.

CERTAINTY CONCERNING FORGIVENESS AND SALVATION

Assurance may come immediately, the moment the soul trusts God, gradually, or a little while after the great spiritual transaction.

It may come in varying degrees, for some may have an instant, strong knowledge of God's acceptance, and others may have a much weaker grasp to begin with.

It may be sensed in different ways. For instance, if two men were standing on railway tracks and a train came suddenly upon them, they would leap out of its path. One man might laugh with joy, but the other might tremble with shock. They had the same deliverance but experienced it differently. It is the prerogative of the Holy Spirit to bring the certainty of sins forgiven, of the new birth and of acceptance with God, however he does it.

No person can do the work of the Spirit in his or her own strength, for this will bring about shallow and spurious fruit. Counsellors are not to tell seekers that they are saved; that is the work of the Holy Spirit! We cannot forcefully bundle seekers in, in an attempt to 'get them saved'. We can and must present the way clearly and scripturally, urging them to receive the Saviour, but when they trust him, perhaps with our help and guidance, it is God who assures them by the inward witness that he has come and that they are saved.

RESULTANT JOY AND STRENGTH

Loving and believing God brings great joy: 'whom having not seen you love. Though now you do not see Him, yet believing, you rejoice with joy inexpressible and full of glory' (1 Peter 1:8); 'for the kingdom of God is not eating and drinking, but righteousness and peace and joy in the Holy Spirit' (Rom. 14:17). There is no doubt about it that the early church knew themselves to be in the kingdom of God. They were saved and they knew it! They did not need to analyse themselves to death to discover their state of grace. They had met with God and this great encounter brought irrepressible joy and amazing strength. They were able to resist persecution in a spirit unheard of before. No one took from them their joy.

RESULTANT POSITIVENESS AND COGENCY OF TESTIMONY

There was nothing uncertain about the response of the man born blind to whom Christ gave sight (John 9). He said, 'One thing I know: that though I was blind, now I see' (v. 25). There was nothing uncertain about Daniel's three friends before they were cast into the fiery furnace: they confidently declared, 'our God ... is able ... [W]e do not serve your gods, nor will we worship the gold image which you have set up' (Dan. 3:18). Those who know God speak with an authority which is born from assurance. Indefinite testimony springs from indefinite experience.

Those who know nothing of assurance are sometimes annoyed by the assured testimony of those in grace and they may criticize or oppose, yet they cannot halt the testimony which streams from an overflowing heart!

RESULTANT SPIRITUAL ILLUMINATION

'However, when He, the Spirit of truth, has come, He will guide you into all truth' (John 16:13). The Holy Spirit reveals truths and illuminates his own work: he not only works in us all kinds of good, but he also shines upon his own work and shows that what he has done is a genuine work of God. Paul says that one great end of our receiving the Spirit is that we may 'know the things that have been freely given to us by God' (1 Cor. 2:12).

Such illumination consciously enriches the trusting soul and is a promise of great things to come. God's secrets are revealed and treasured as the Spirit illumines and witnesses in the hearts of those who abide in God. The precious truths of God await our patient search.

A final challenge

The Bible says, in its best-known verse, 'For God so loved the world that He gave His only begotten Son, that whoever believes in Him should not perish but have everlasting life' (John 3:16). The gift of God was his Son.

It also says that 'as many as received Him, to them He gave the right to become children of God' (John 1:12). The gift of God's Son is to be received!

In 1 John 5:12 we read, 'He who has the Son has life.' If we have received the Son, God says that we have life! And to confirm it, he says, 'These things I have written to you who believe [or trust] in the name of the Son of God, that you may know that you have eternal life' (1 John 5:13). That's what God says!

Our salvation is to be based not on feelings, but on the Word of God. That cannot fail.

Christ confirms this by saying, 'he who hears My word and believes in Him who sent me has everlasting life, and shall not come into judgment, but has passed from death into life' (John 5:24). To believe is not merely to give an intellectual assent to spiritual truth, but it is to trust in, rely on and cling to God's Word as you receive God's Son; 'he who believes in Me [trusts in Me, relies on Me, clings to Me]', says Jesus, 'has everlasting life' (John 6:47). It is a present possession! It happens now! What a wonderful moment: the moment when I trust Jesus to forgive my sins, to come into my heart and to make me his child!

God comes to dwell in me! Deity indwelling humanity! How very wonderful! Truly we can sing,

He lives! He lives! Christ Jesus lives today!
He walks with me and talks with me along life's narrow way.
He lives! He lives! Salvation to impart;
You ask me how I know he lives?
He lives within my heart!
(A. H. Ackley).

You see, I don't have to go to the library or university and plough through all the religious volumes to find out whether Jesus lives. I know! He lives within my heart! There is an inner assurance, an inner witness! The Spirit witnesses with my spirit that I am his child. Amen and amen!

The church has sung for years,

Blessèd assurance, Jesus is mine!
Oh, what a foretaste of glory divine!
Heir of salvation, purchase of God,
Born of his Spirit, washed in his blood.
This is my story, this is my song,
Praising my Saviour all the day long …
(Fanny J. Crosby, 1820–1915).

Believers know that they are heirs of salvation; they know that they are purchased of God; they know that they are born of God's Spirit; they know that they are washed in Christ's blood. This surely is their story and this is their song! Blessed assurance indeed!

Many years ago in the USA, a slave lad came under deep conviction of sin. His mistress noticed his distress and became very concerned about him. Eventually she spoke to him and discovered his trouble. She sought to comfort him by telling him that he must have experienced religion because he did nothing wicked. To this he replied, 'No, madam, I don't want that kind of religion that I can have and not know it, 'cause I might lose it and not miss it.'

Have you had an experience that you know about? Do you know that you are Christ's? Does the Spirit of God witness with your spirit that you are a child of God? Can you say with complete certainty, 'Blessed assurance, Jesus is mine'? This surely is our great scriptural heritage, our enormous spiritual privilege and our inestimable joy.

Notes

1   **Bruce Milne,** *Know the Truth* (Leicester: IVP, 1982), p. 192.
2   **J. D. Douglas** (ed.), *The New Bible Dictionary* (London: IVP, 1962), p. 100.
3   **John Calvin,** *Institutes of the Christian Religion*, vol. i (Grand Rapids, MI: Eerdmans [date unknown]), pp. 71–72.
4   **Louis Berkhof,** *Systematic Theology* (Edinburgh: Banner of Truth, 1939), p. 507.
5   **Ray Stedman,** *Expository Studies in 2 Corinthians* (Palo Alto, CA: Word, 1982) [page unknown].
6   **C. H. Spurgeon,** *Treasury of the New Testament*, vol. iv (London: Marshall, Morgan & Scott, n.d.), p. 611.
7   **J. Agar Beet,** *Commentary on Paul's Epistles*, quoted in **Mark J. Rich,** 'Are You Truly Alive in Christ?', *Online Bible* (Oakhurst, NJ: Software for Macintosh by Ken Hamel, 1995).
8   **J. C. Ryle,** *Assurance* (Fearn: Christian Focus, 1992), p. 21.
9   **Merrill C. Tenney** (ed.), *Zondervan's Pictorial Bible Dictionary* (Grand Rapids, MI: Zondervan, 1963), p. 78.
10 **Ernest S. Williams,** *Systematic Theology*, vol. ii (Springfield, MO: Gospel Publishing House, 1953), p. 289.

11 Sinclair B. Ferguson, David F. Wright, J. I. Packer (eds.), *New Dictionary of Theology* (Leicester: IVP, 1988), p. 51.

12 D. MacLeod, *A Faith to Live By* (Fearn: Christian Focus, 2002), p. 185.

13 D. D. Whedon, *Commentaries*, vol. v (1880; 1978, Salem, OH: Schmul Publishers), p. 279.

14 *The Westminster Shorter Catechism*, q. 36: 'What are the benefits which in this life do accompany or flow from justification, adoption, and sanctification?'

15 Quoted in **W. J. Townsend, H. B. Workman and G. Eayers,** *A New History of Methodism*, vol. i (London: Hodder & Stoughton, 1909), p. 23.

16 Quoted in **A. S. Yates,** *The Doctrine of Assurance* (London: Epworth Press, 1952), p. 171.

17 Quoted in **T. C. Mitchell,** *Mr Wesley* (Kansas City, MO: Beacon Hill, 1957), p. 40.

18 George Whitefield, Sermon 38, 'The Indwelling of the Spirit, the common Privilege of all Believers' in *Selected Sermons*; quoted in **Mark J. Rich,** *Are You Truly Alive in Christ? Online Bible* (Oakhurst, NJ: Software for Macintosh by Ken Hamel, 1995).

19 Quoted in **Yates,** *Doctrine of Assurance*, p. 172.

20 John Wesley, *Works*, vol. iii (London: John Mason, 1829), p. 369.

21 Quoted in **S. Banks,** *Our Wesleyan Heritage* (unpublished MS from Emmanuel Bible College, Birkenhead), p. 19.

22 Quoted in **Banks,** *Our Wesleyan Heritage*, p. 27.

23 John Wesley, *A Plain Account of Christian Perfection* (London: Epworth Press, 1952), p. 45.

24 From **Wesley's** letters, quoted in **M. James** (ed.), *The Flame*, Jan./Feb. 1975, p. 34.

25 Quoted in **L. G. Cox,** *John Wesley's Concept of Christian Perfection* (Kansas City, MO: Beacon Hill, 1964), p. 88.

26 Wesley, *Works*, vol. vi, pp. 5–6.

27 Ibid. p. 509.

28 Ibid. pp. 52–53.

29 Ibid. vol. xii, pp. 393–400.

30 Ibid. vol. xiv, pp. 270–271.

31 *Book of Common Prayer*, General Confession.

About Day One:

Day One's threefold commitment:

- To be faithful to the Bible, God's inerrant, infallible Word;
- To be relevant to our modern generation;
- To be excellent in our publication standards.

I continue to be thankful for the publications of Day One. They are biblical; they have sound theology; and they are relative to the issues at hand. The material is condensed and manageable while, at the same time, being complete—a challenging balance to find. We are happy in our ministry to make use of these excellent publications.

JOHN MACARTHUR, PASTOR-TEACHER, GRACE COMMUNITY CHURCH, CALIFORNIA

It is a great encouragement to see Day One making such excellent progress. Their publications are always biblical, accessible and attractively produced, with no compromise on quality. Long may their progress continue and increase!

JOHN BLANCHARD, AUTHOR, EVANGELIST AND APOLOGIST

Visit our web site for more information and to request a free catalogue of our books.

www.dayone.co.uk

Exploring Jushua:
A devotional commentary

COLIN PECKHAM

240 PAGES PAPERBACK

978–1–84625–093–4

E ploring
THE BIBLE

Joshua
A devotional commentary

Colin N Peckham

Day One

Joshua—what a book!

It is a necessary bridge between the Law of Moses and the rest of Israel's history.

It magnifies the faithfulness and power of God.

It runs from the epic crossing of the Jordan to the final conquest of the land, this being seen as a vivid and graphic picture of claiming our rich inheritance in Christ.

It shows that they could only get into the land of victory and fullness through crossing Jordan, the 'river of death', this being a picture of our dying with Christ and rising with him to a new and abundant resurrection life.

It reveals the reasons for their failures and shows obedience and faith to be the basis for their victories.

Joshua is a very important book in the canon of Scripture and this devotional commentary merits your attention. It will challenge you with penetrating insights into Scripture and into your own heart. That in essence is its objective—to confront men and women with the necessity of integrity, purity and victory through obedience and faith.

If you are looking for a fast moving, down-to-earth and challenging insight into Joshua, then this is it. Colin Peckham presents a grasp of the book that is easy to take in, particularly the long historical chapters, and manages at the same time to show how the book's message is just as vital for today as it has always been. Buy it, study it and act upon it.

—REV. DR A M ROGER, PRINCIPAL, THE FAITH MISSION BIBLE COLLEGE, EDINBURGH

IAIN D CAMPBELL

96PP, ILLUSTRATED PAPERBACK

ISBN 978–1–84625–082–8

What's the big story that ties together all the little stories of the Bible?

In this short book Iain D Campbell tries to answer that question by emphasizing seven key points on which the storyline of the Bible hangs.

These are seven moments of awe-inspiring activity on the part of God in the history of the world, events which revolve around Jesus Christ, whom the Bible portrays as the Saviour we all need.

Rev. Dr Iain D Campbell is pastor of Back Free Church of Scotland on the Isle of Lewis. He trained for the ministry at the University of Glasgow and at the Free Church College Edinburgh. He is married to Anne, a teacher, and they have three children: Iain, Stephen and Emily. Iain is author of three other books published by Day One: On the first day of the week—God, the Christian and the Sabbath, The gospel according to Ruth, and Opening up Exodus.

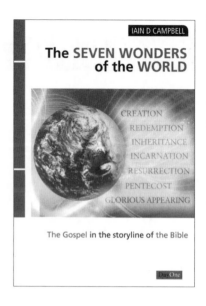

The Gospel in the storyline of the Bible

What an ideal book for a generation which is biblically illiterate, yet fascinated by stories! For Iain Campbell shows how the Bible tells the greatest of all stories—which has moreover the merit of being true. Taken together, these seven highlights of God's saving activity provide a rounded picture of the Person in whom alone salvation is to be found—the Lord Jesus Christ. Dr Campbell has mastered the art of profound simplicity, with a wealth of teaching contained in an accessible and fascinating narrative. 'Wonderful' in more than one sense!

—*EDWARD DONNELLY, MINISTER, TRINITY REFORMED PRESBYTERIAN CHURCH, NEWTOWNABBEY AND PRINCIPAL, REFORMED THEOLOGICAL COLLEGE, BELFAST*